Mandalas

Mandalas

ISBN: 9798633156744

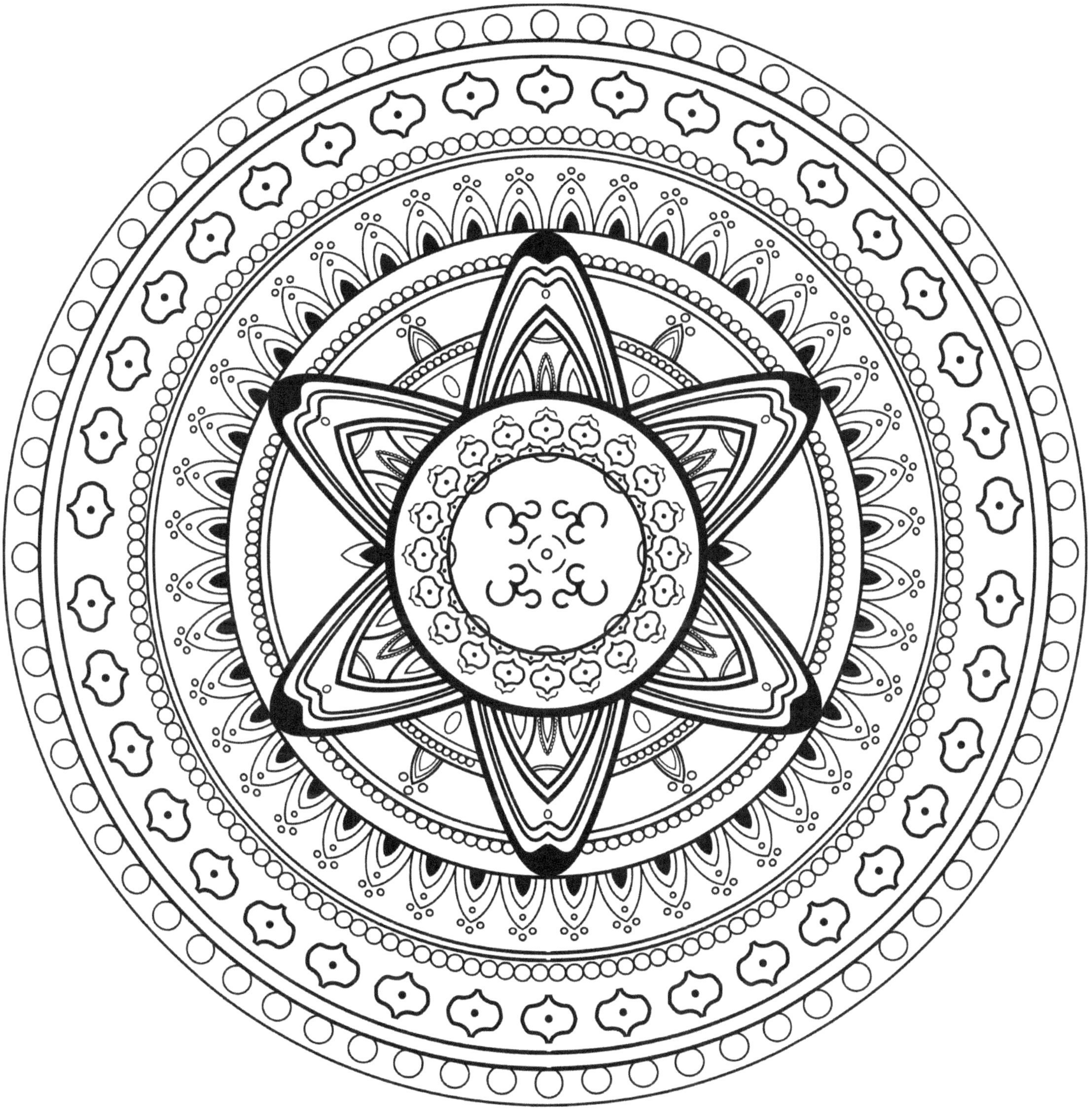

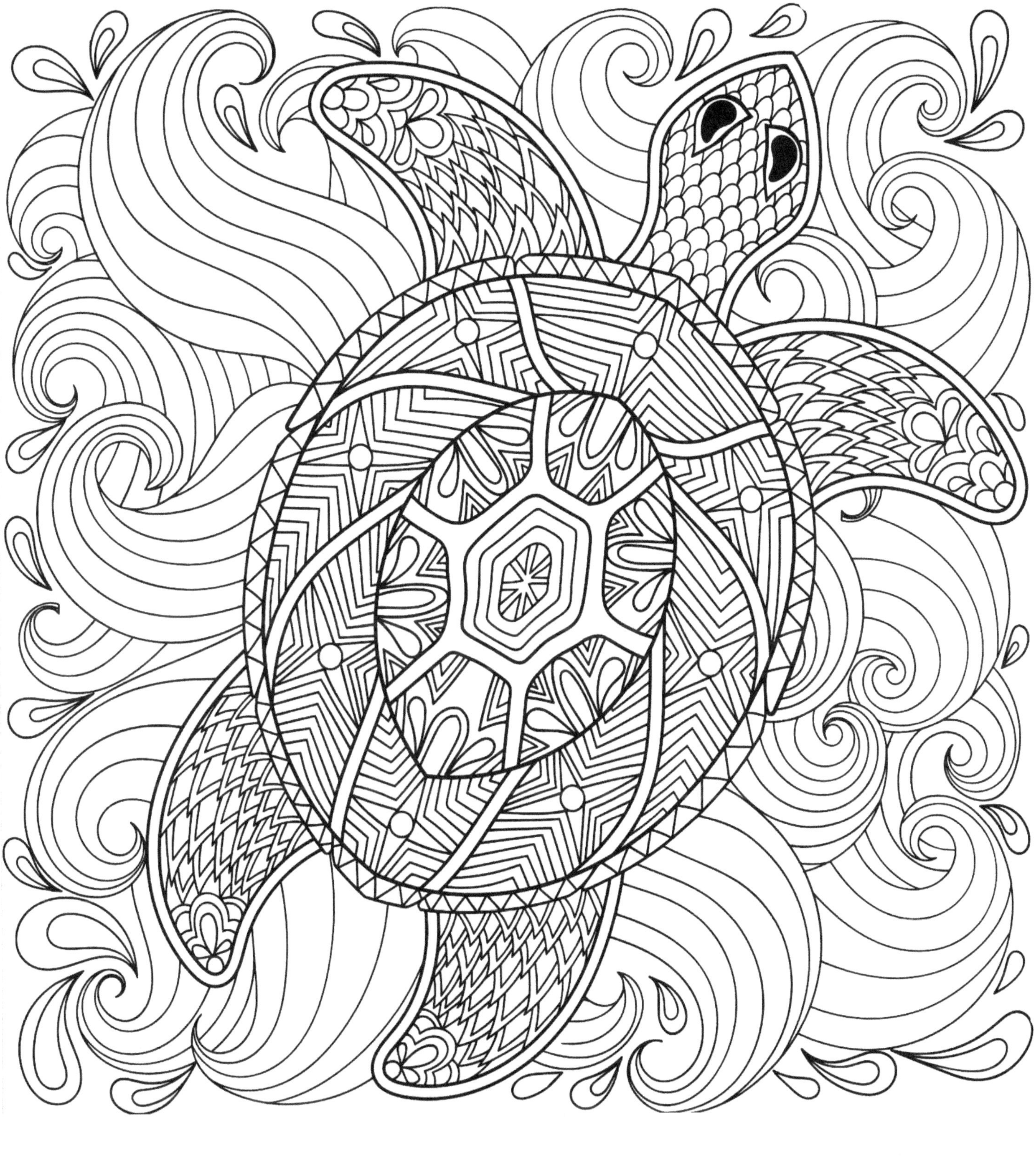

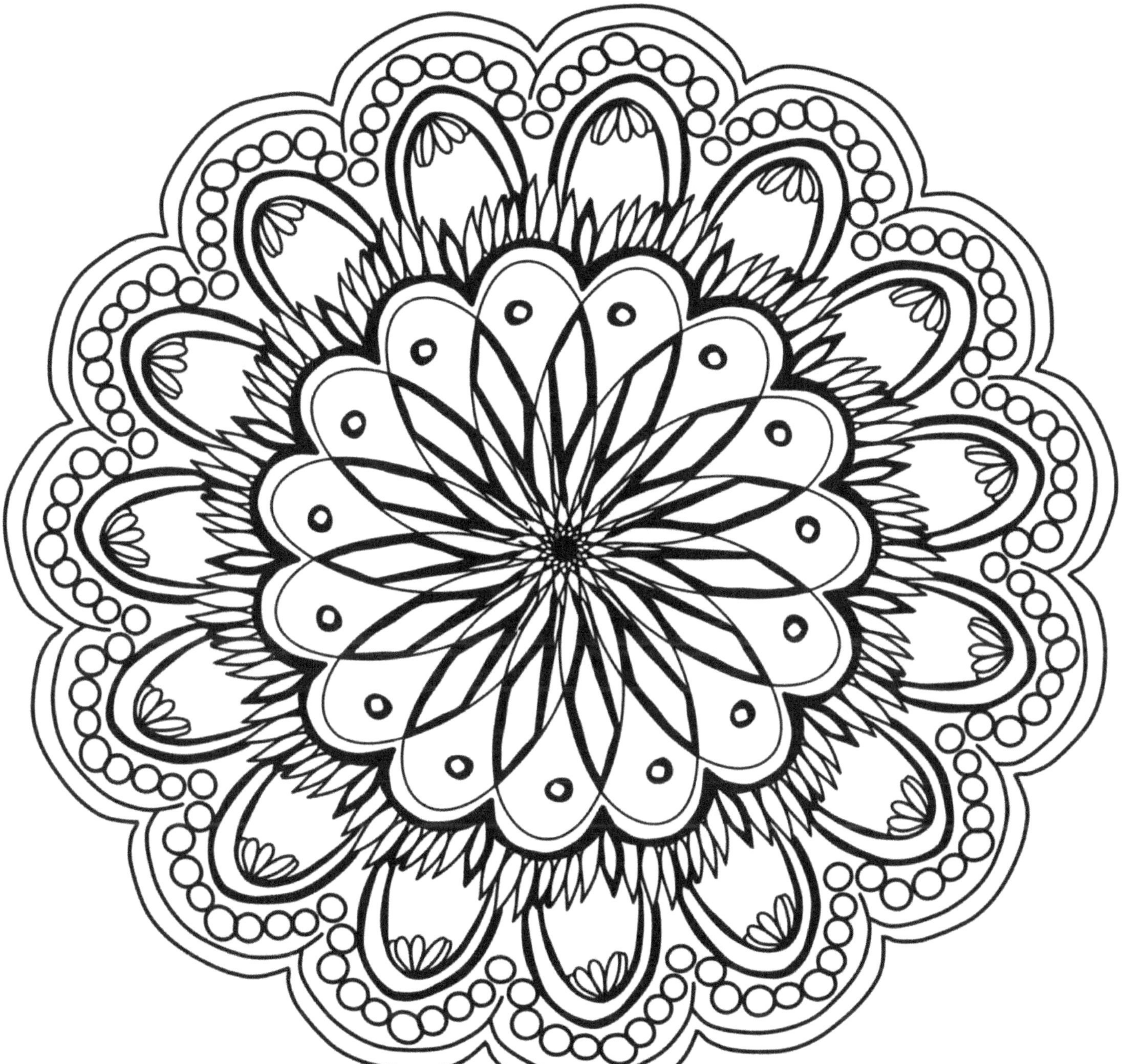

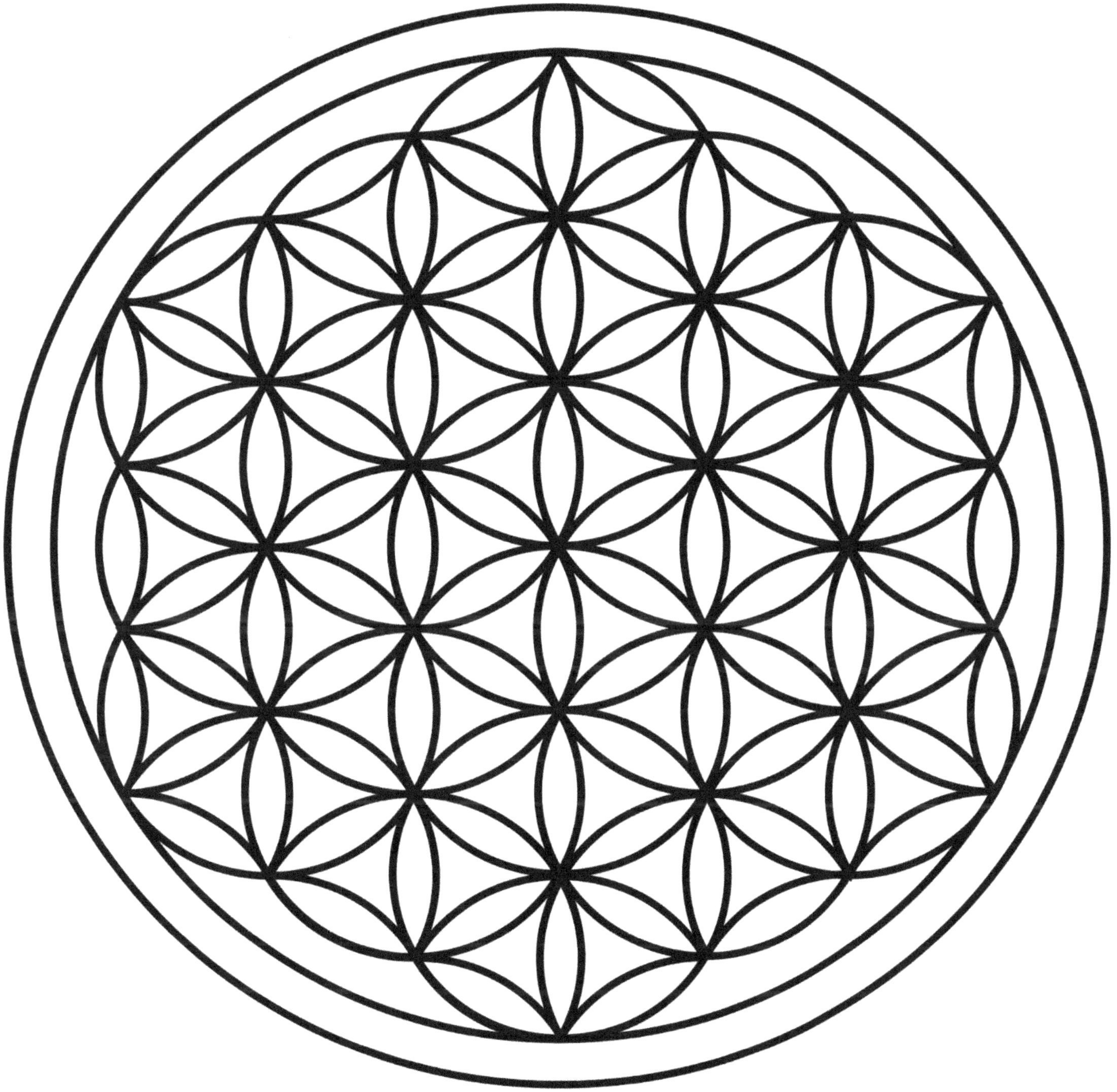

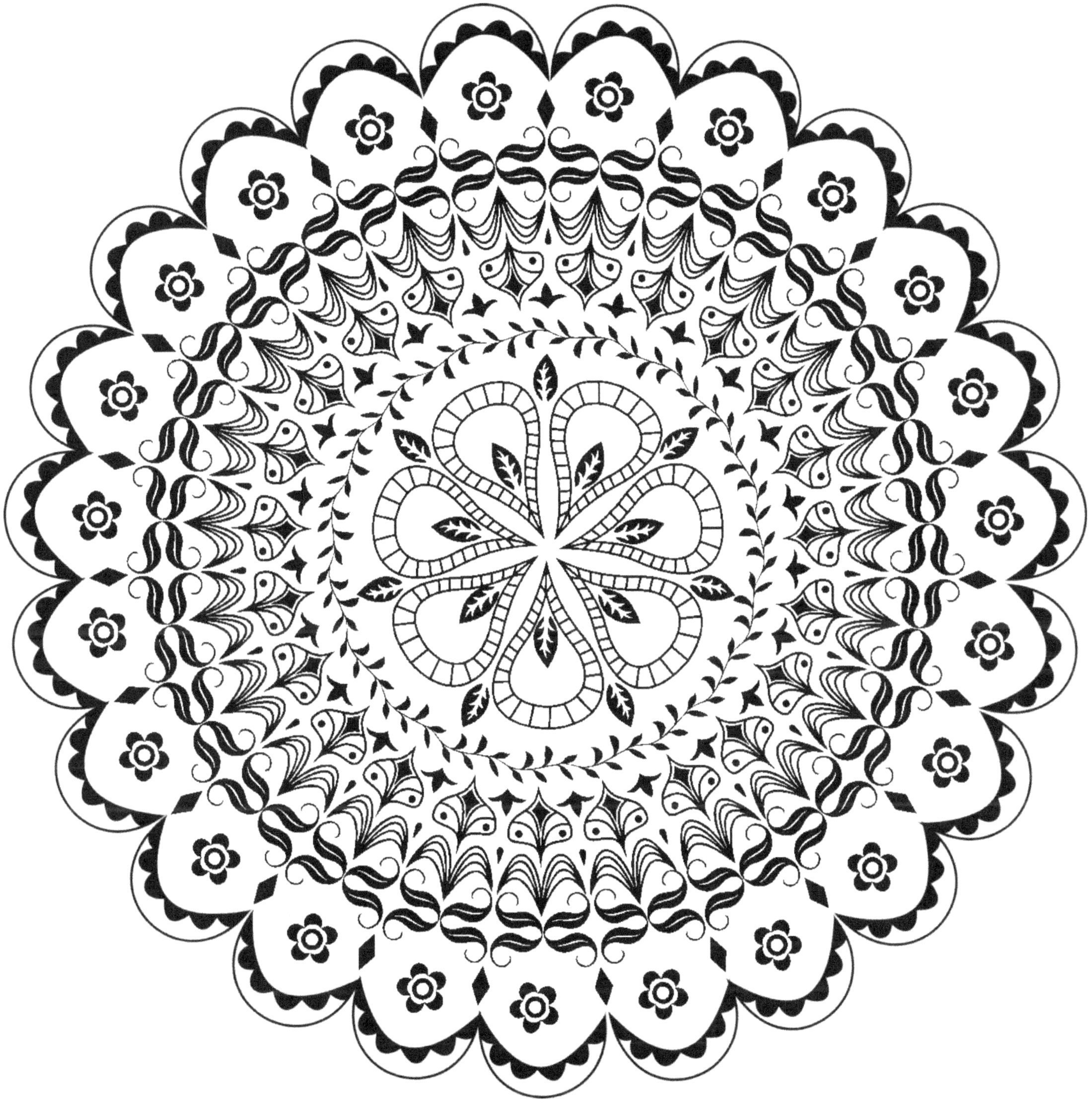

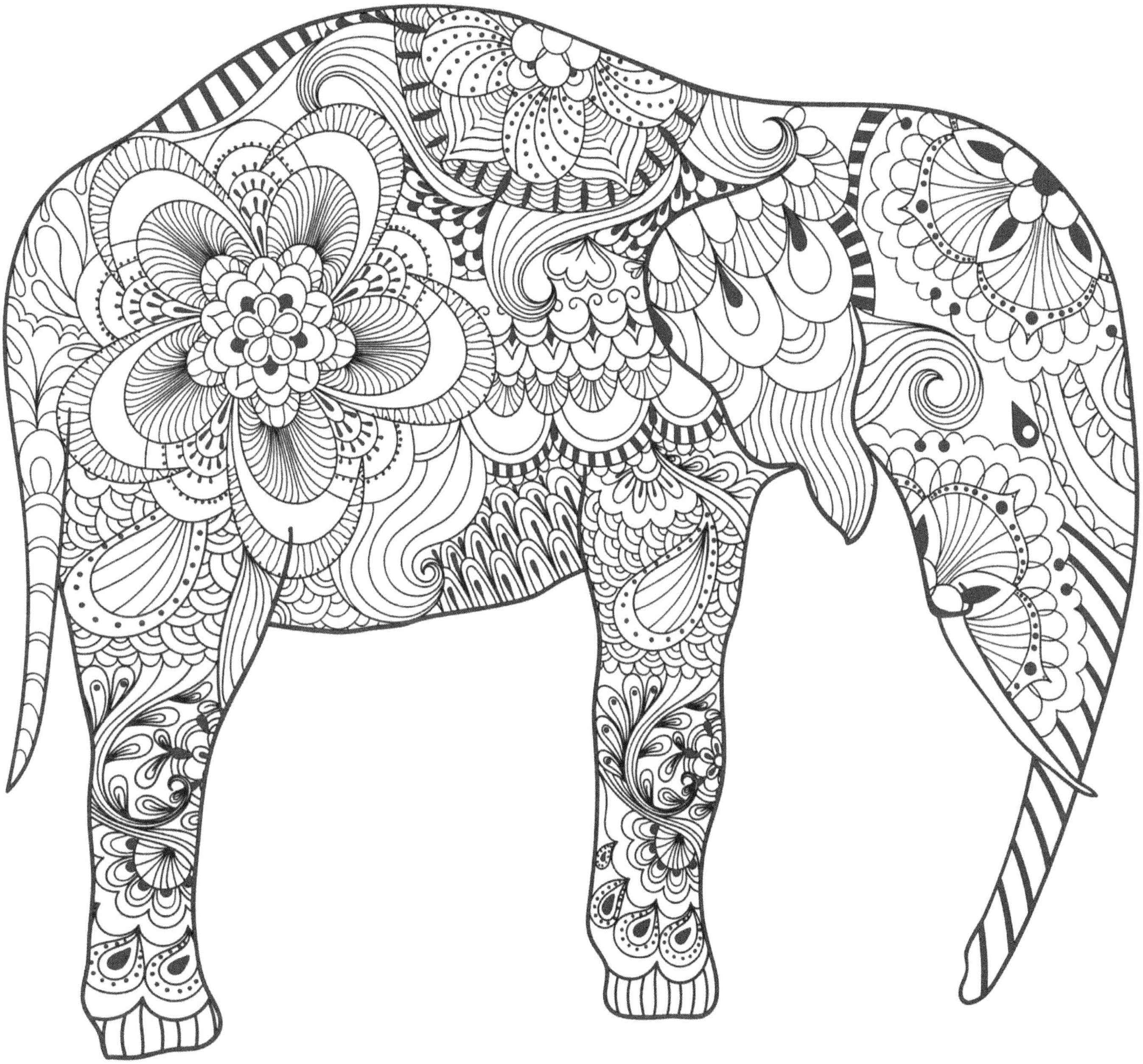

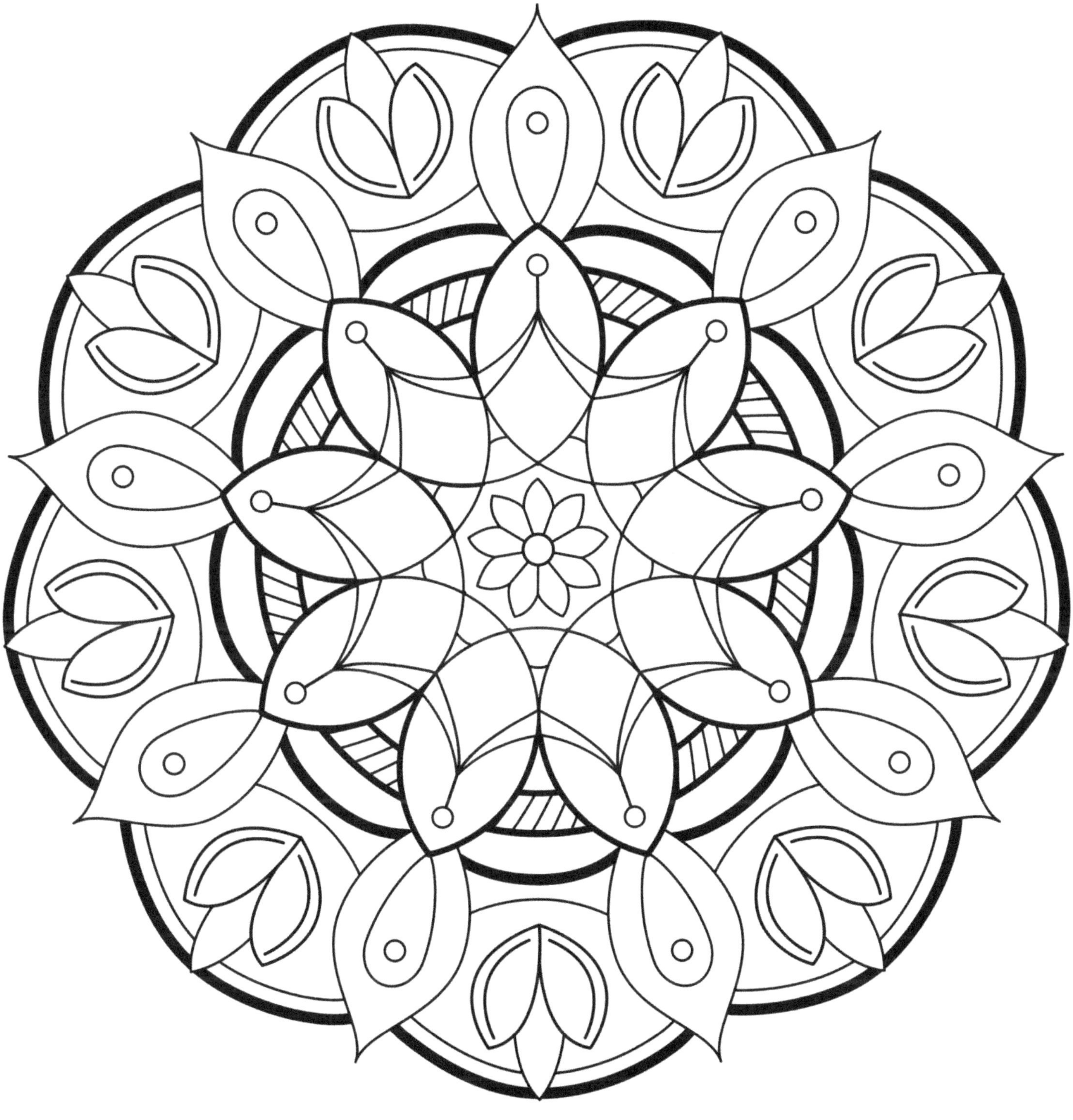

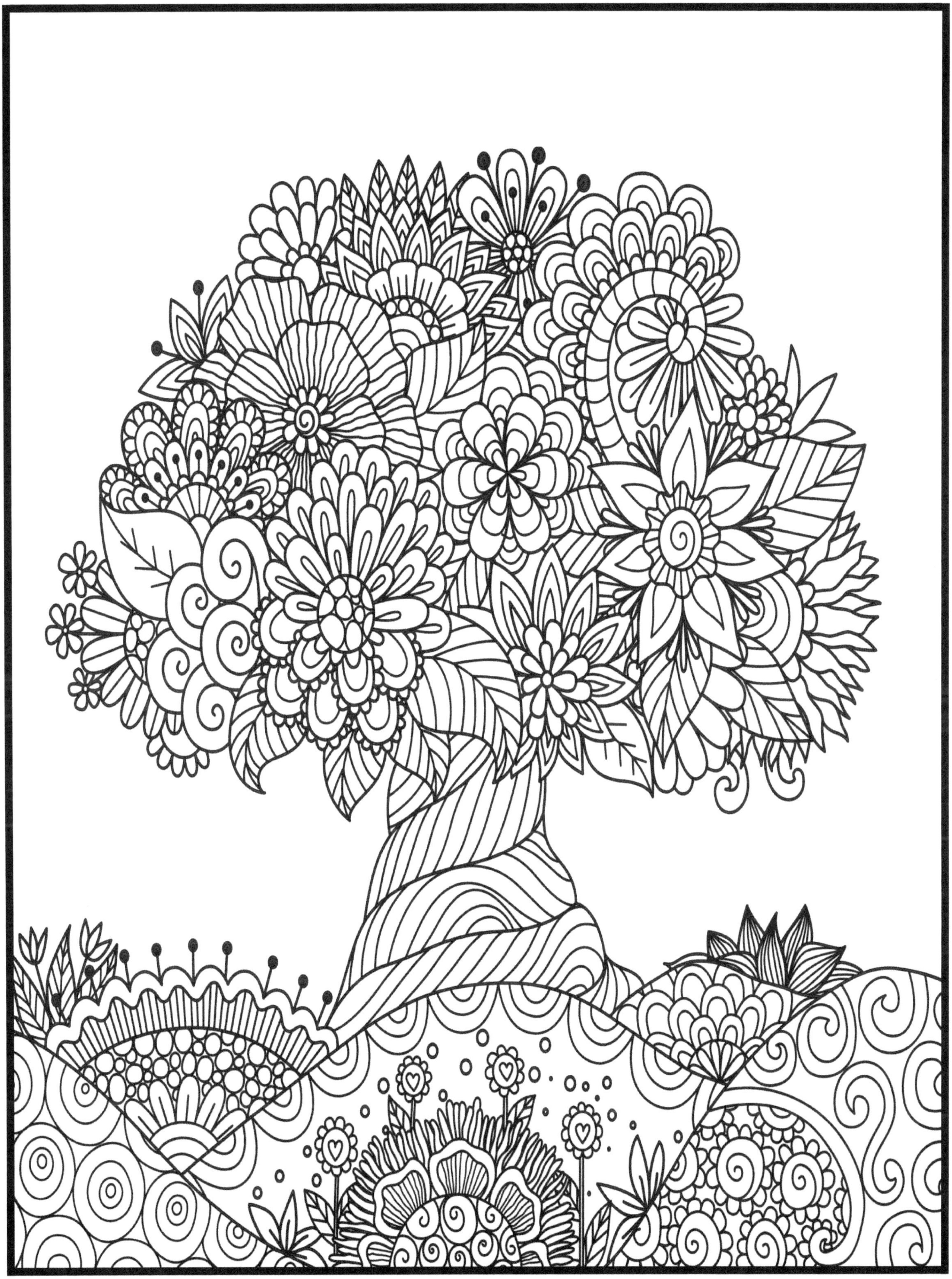

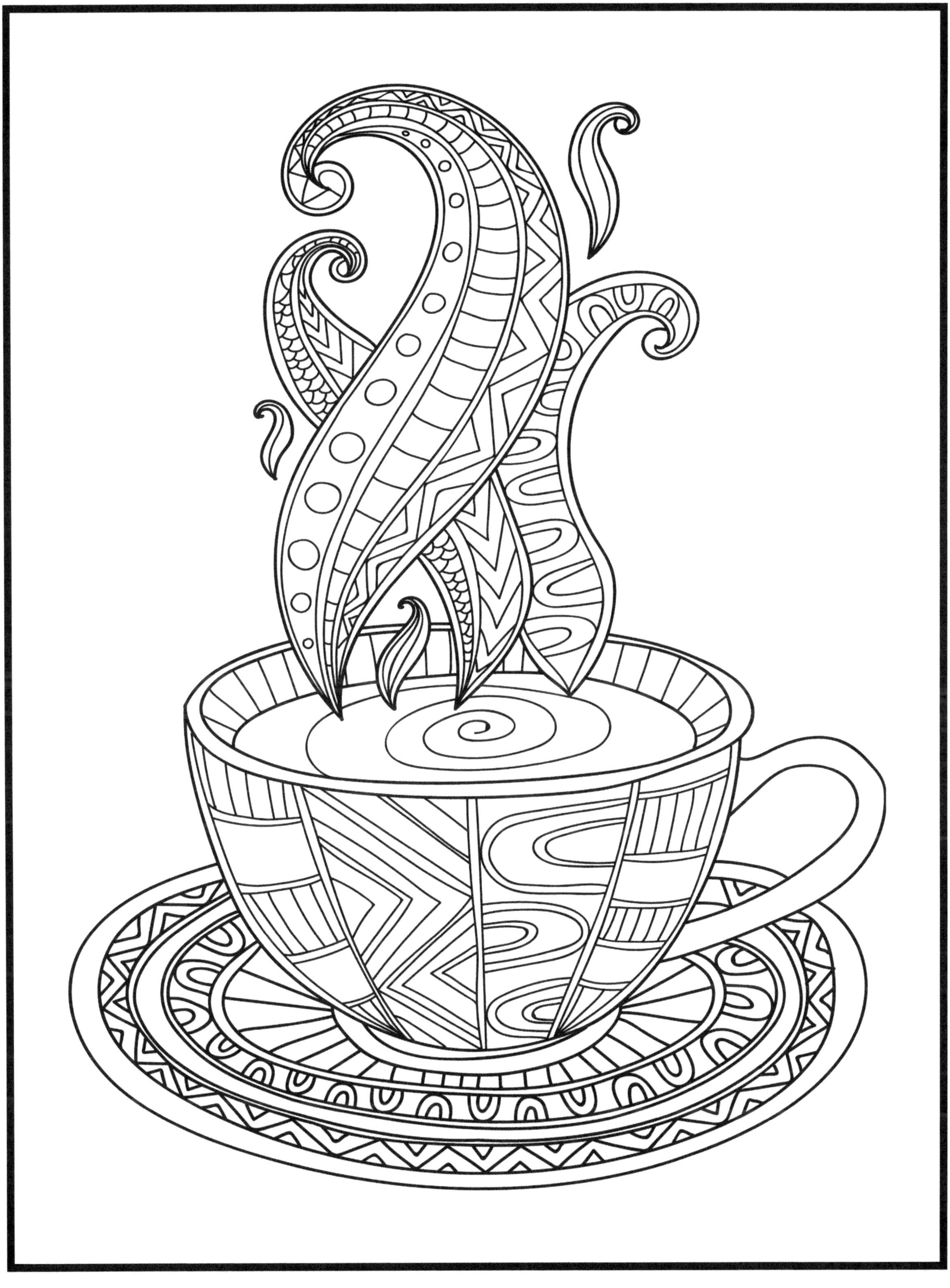

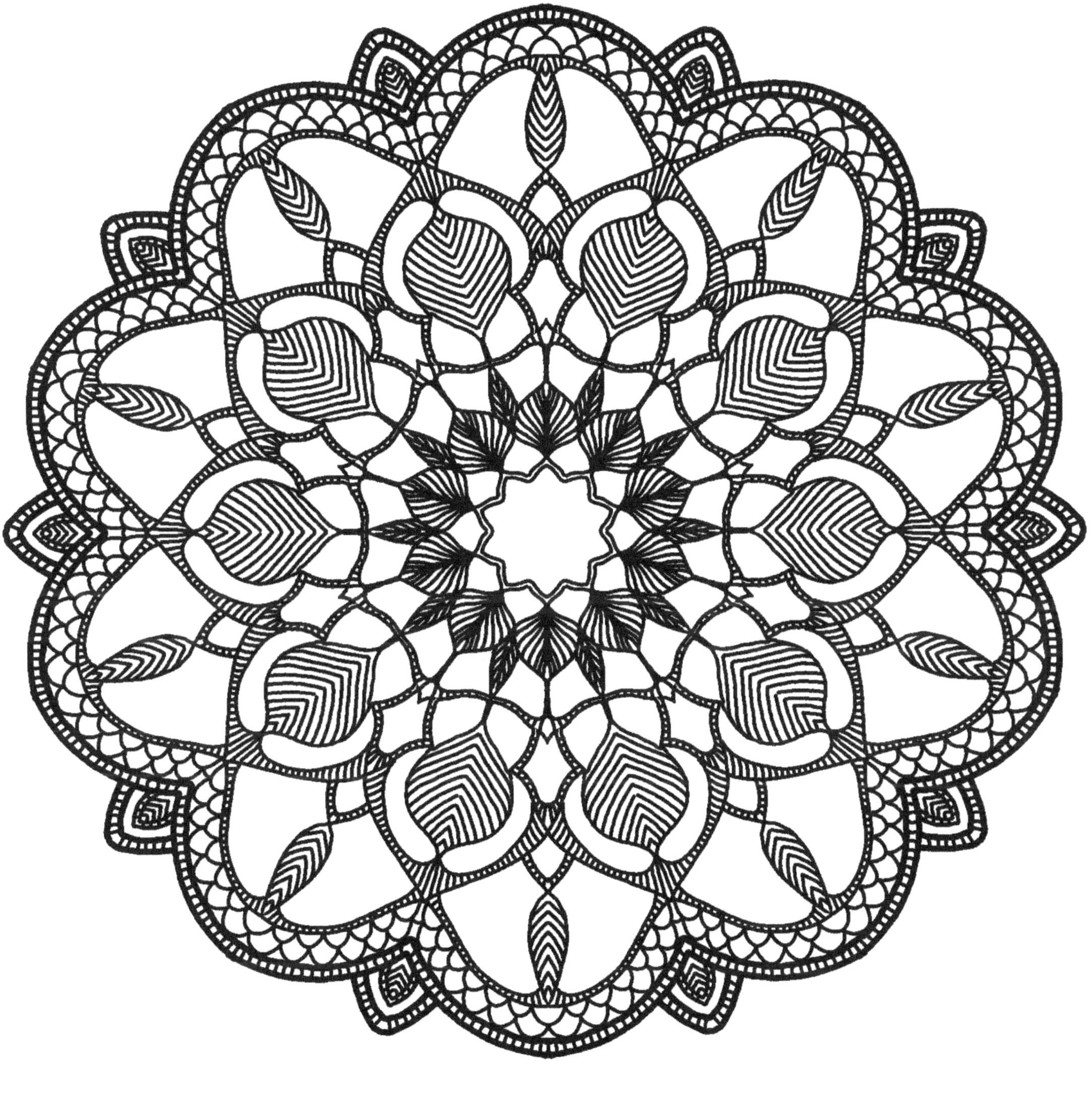

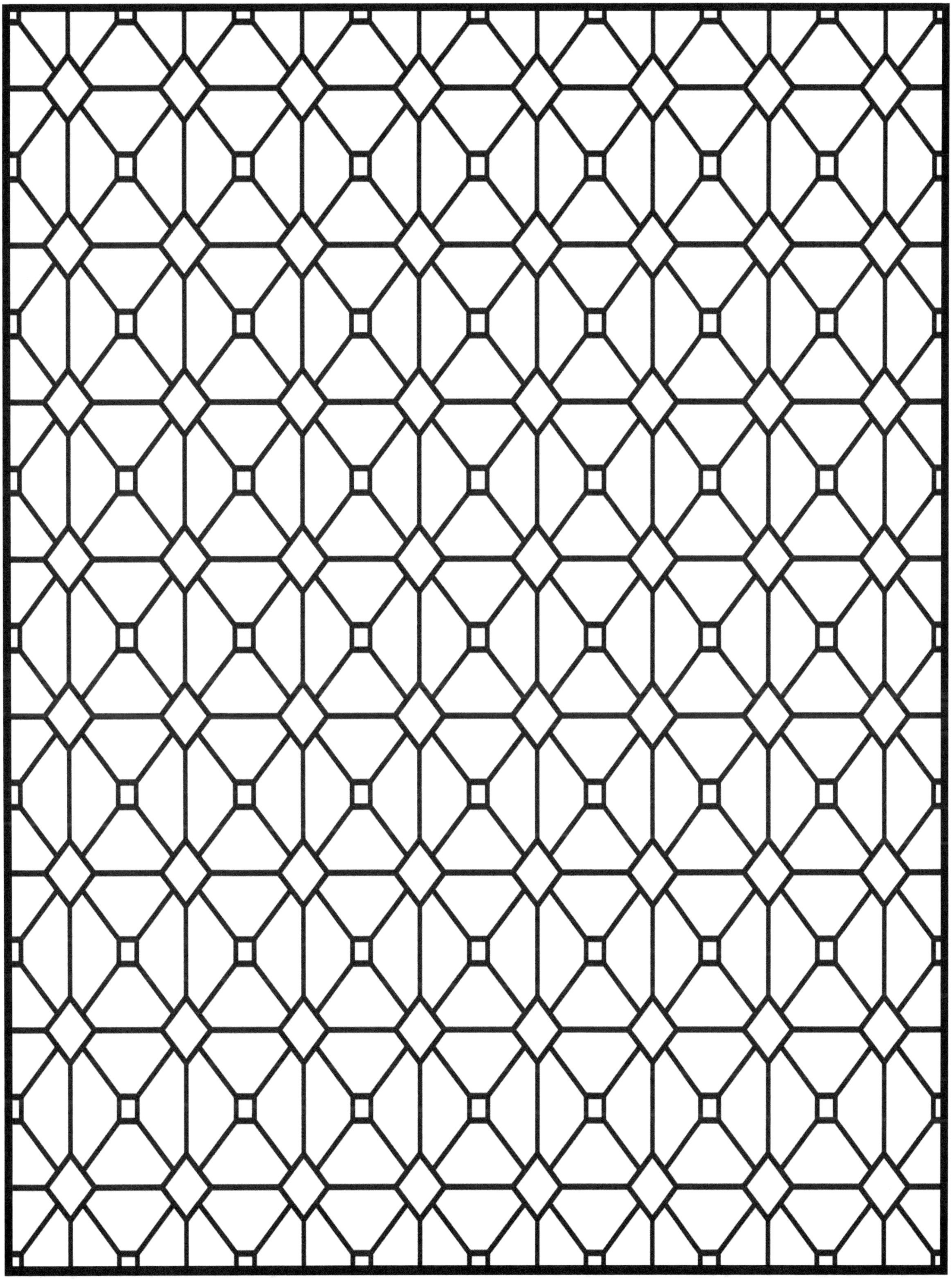

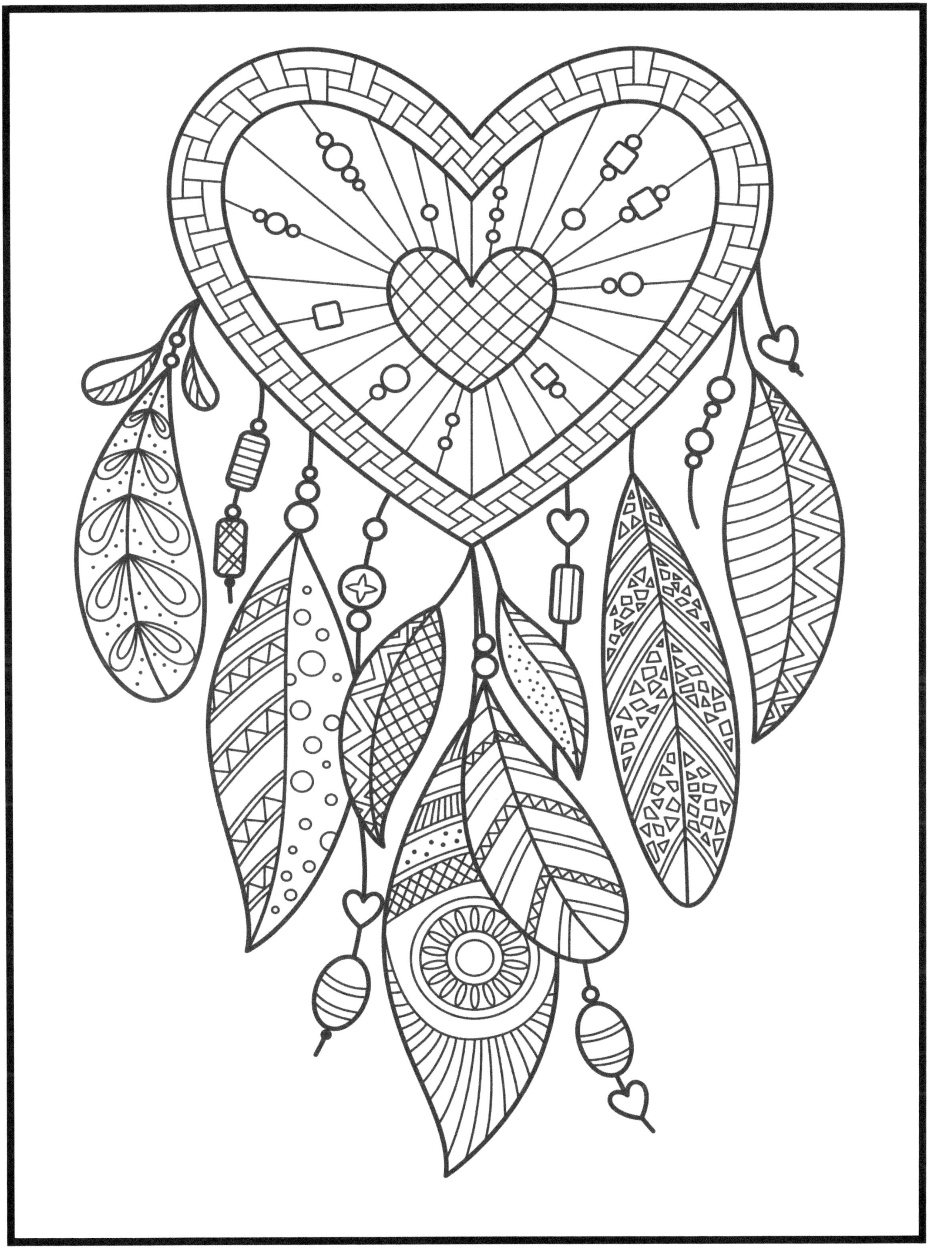

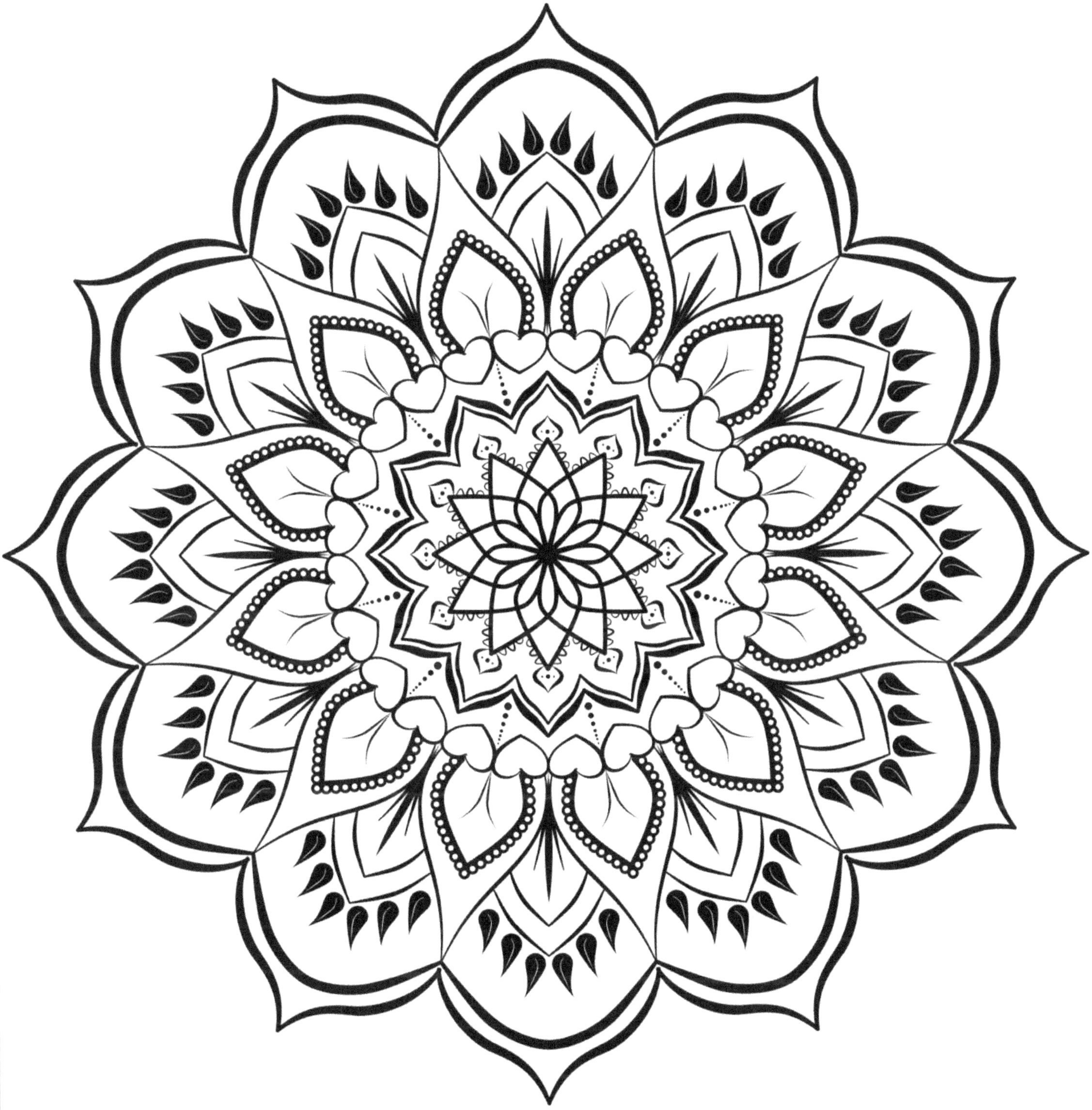

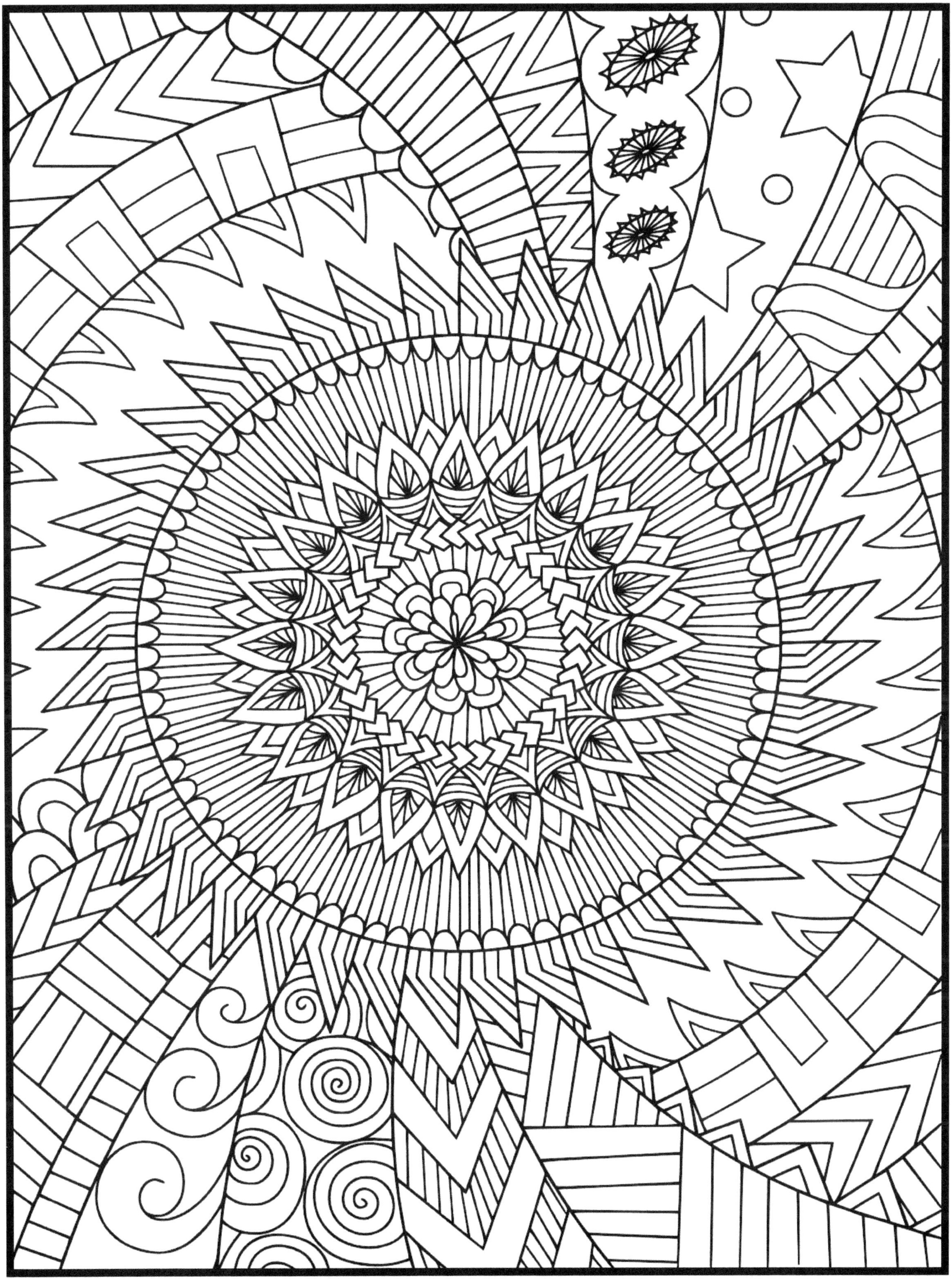

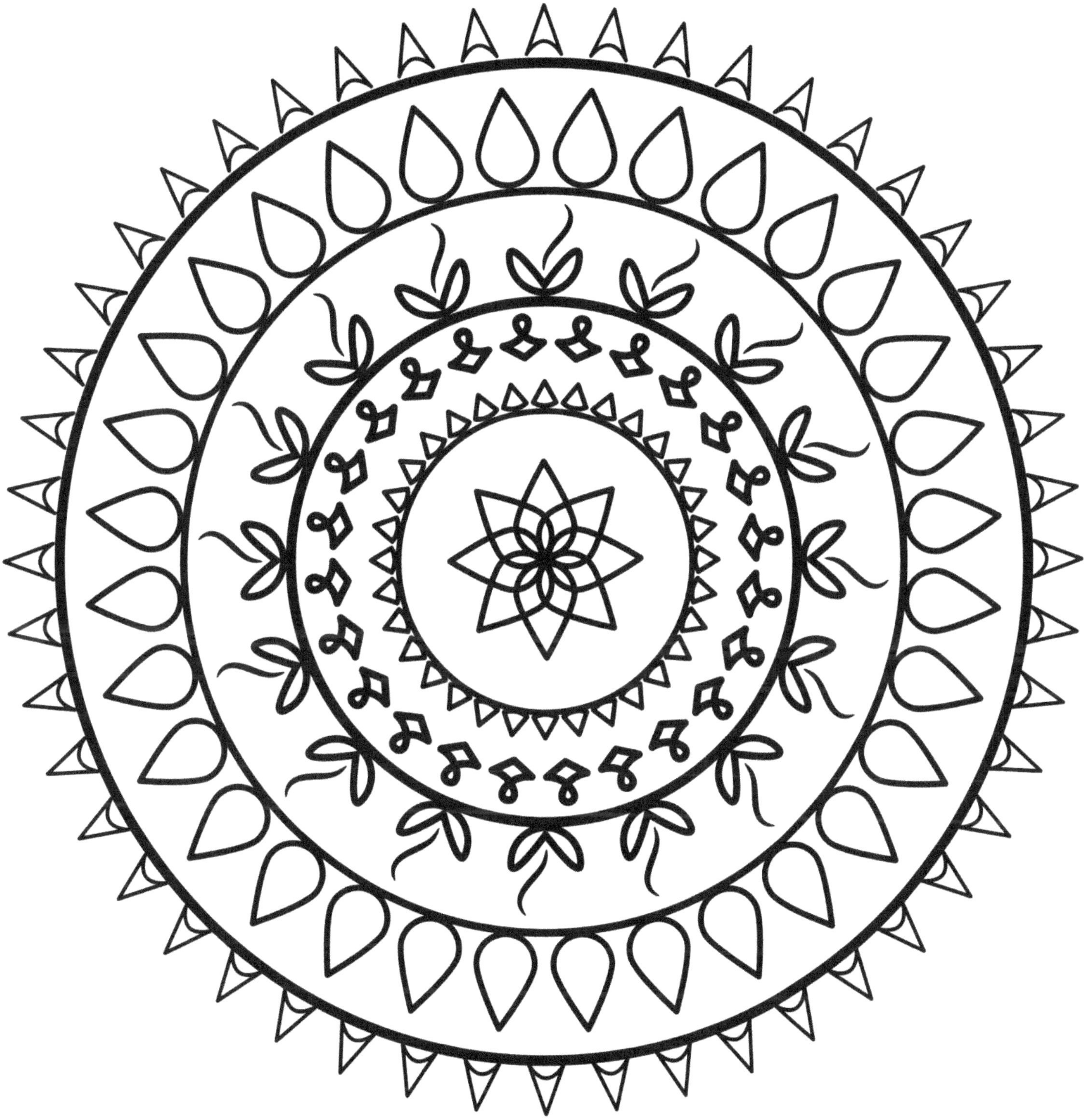

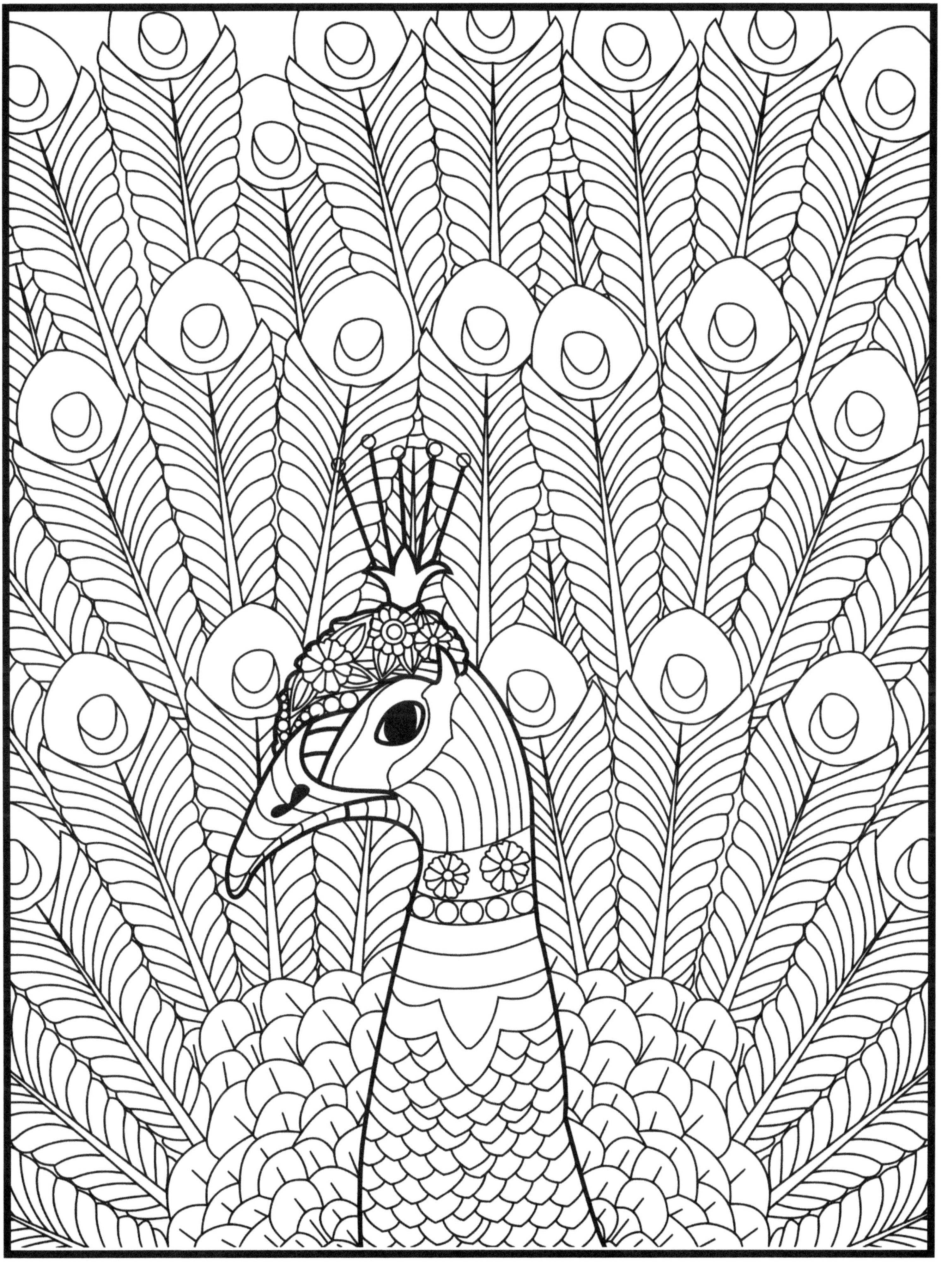

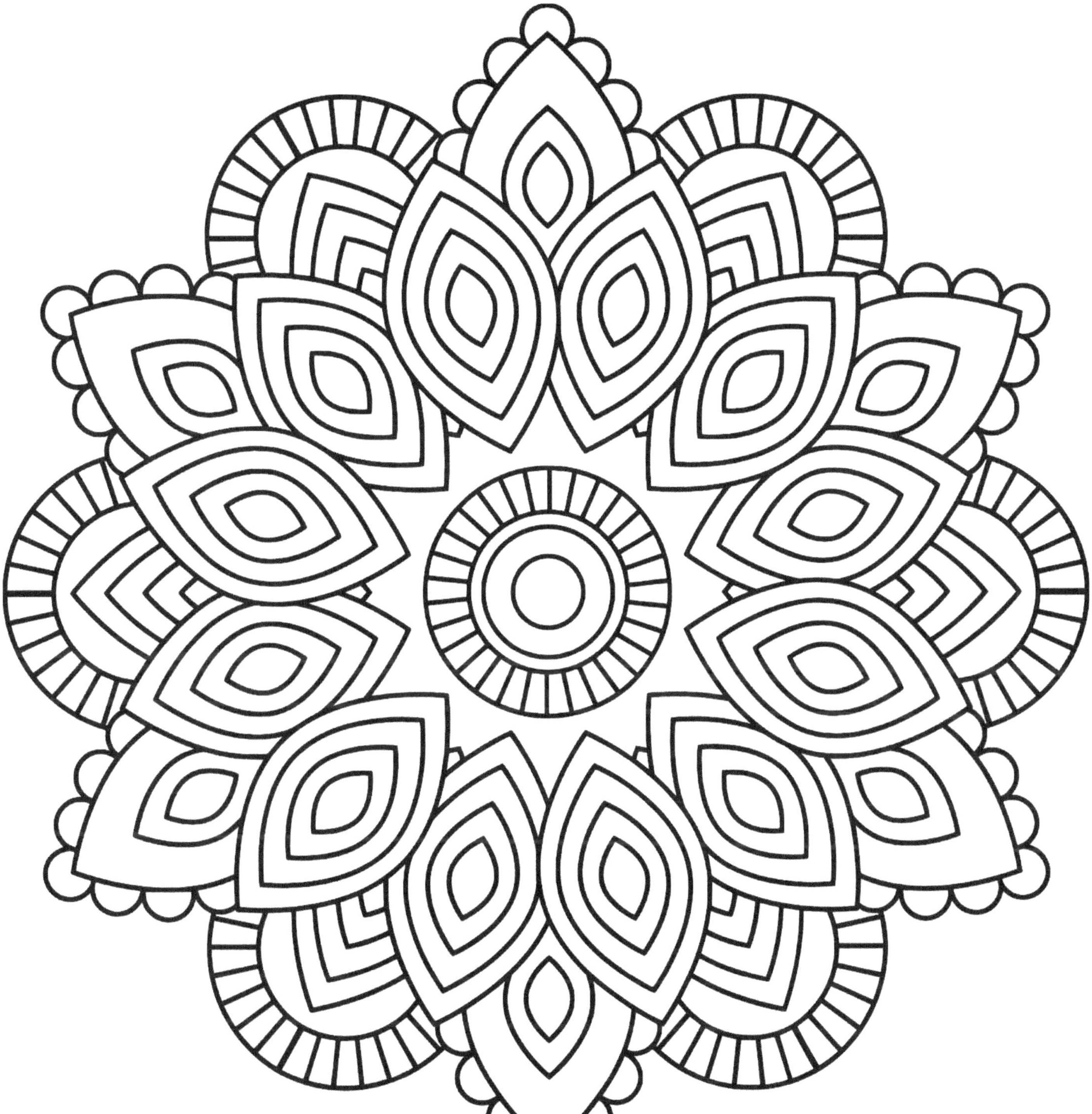

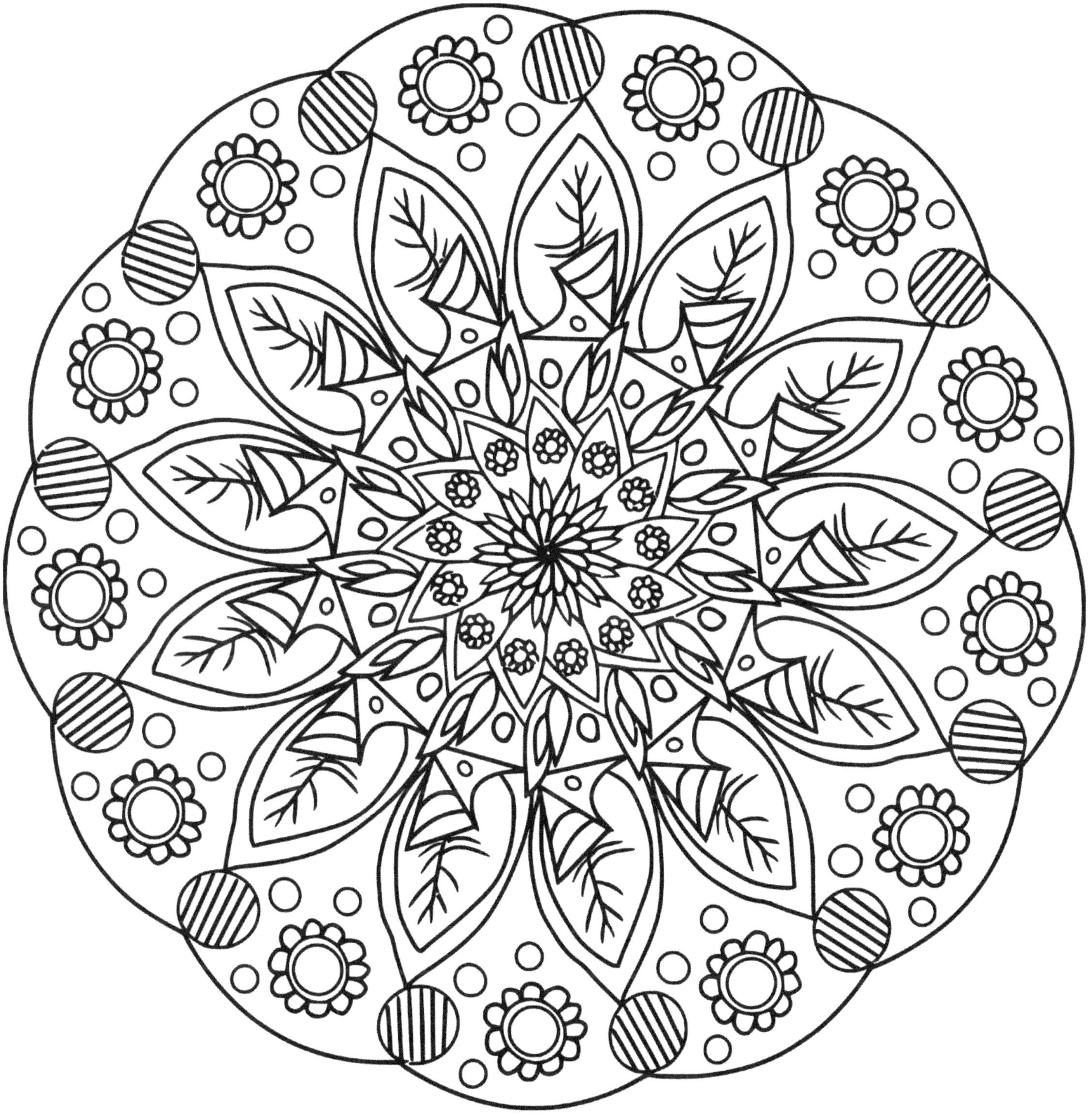

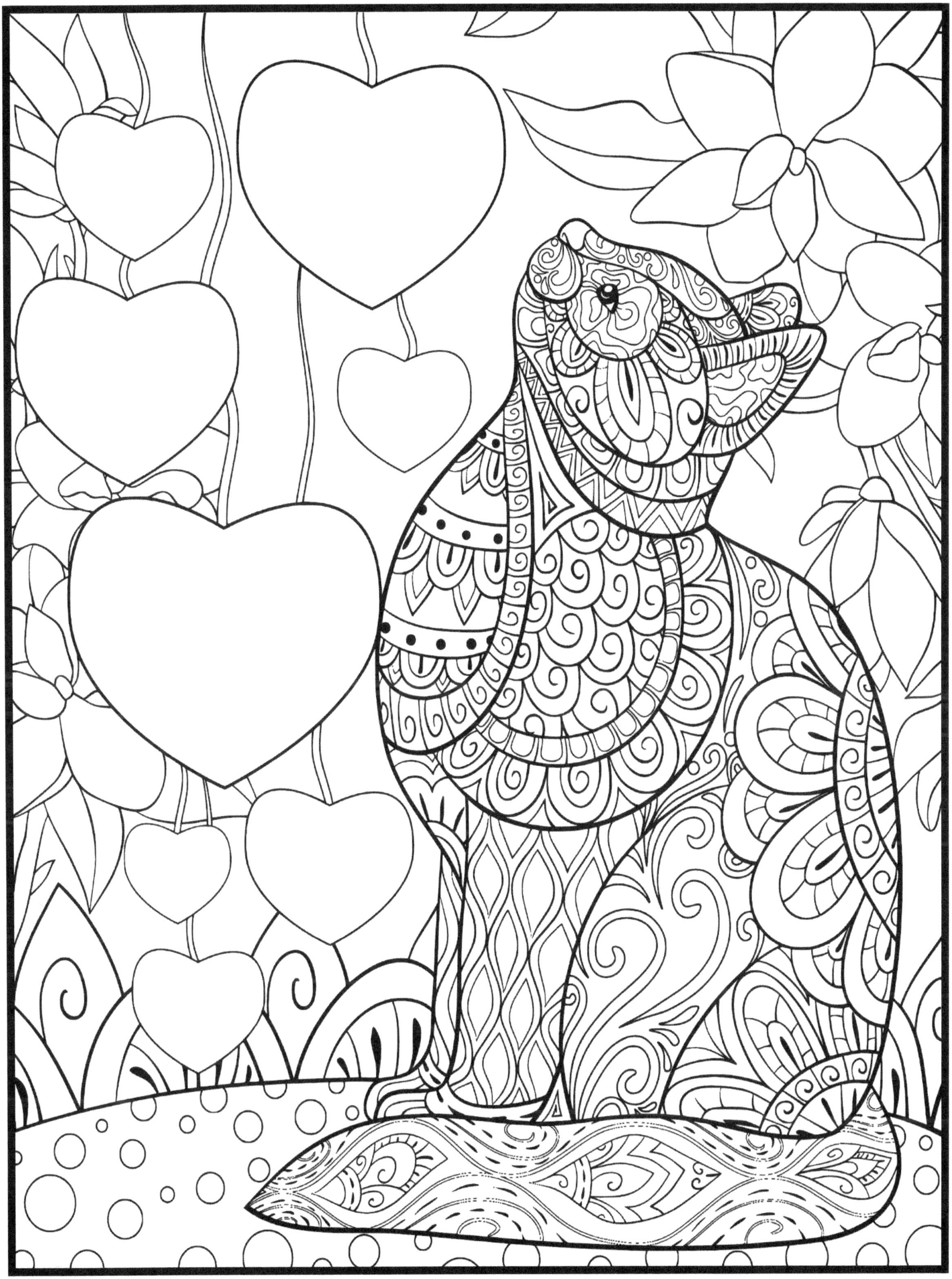

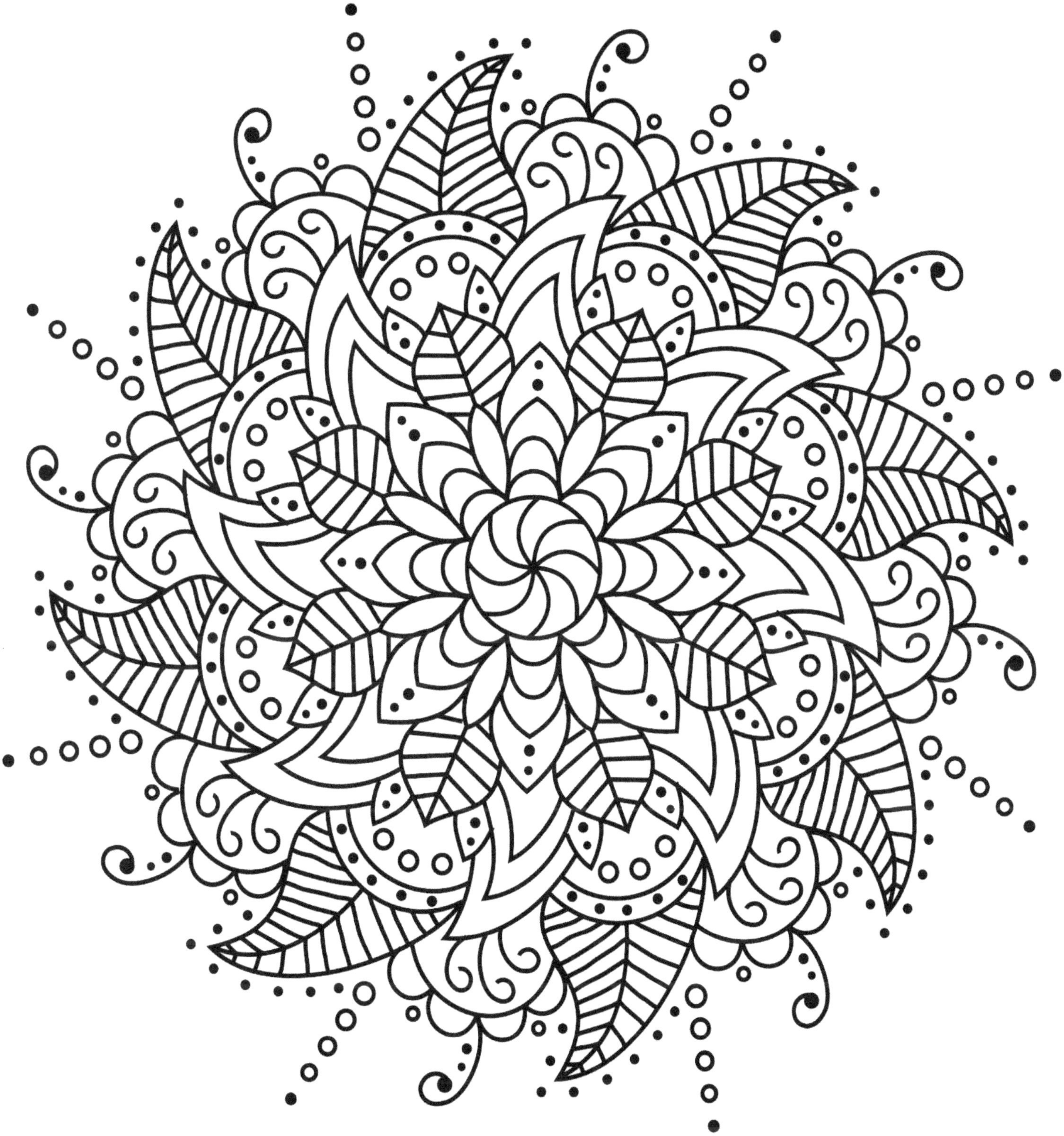

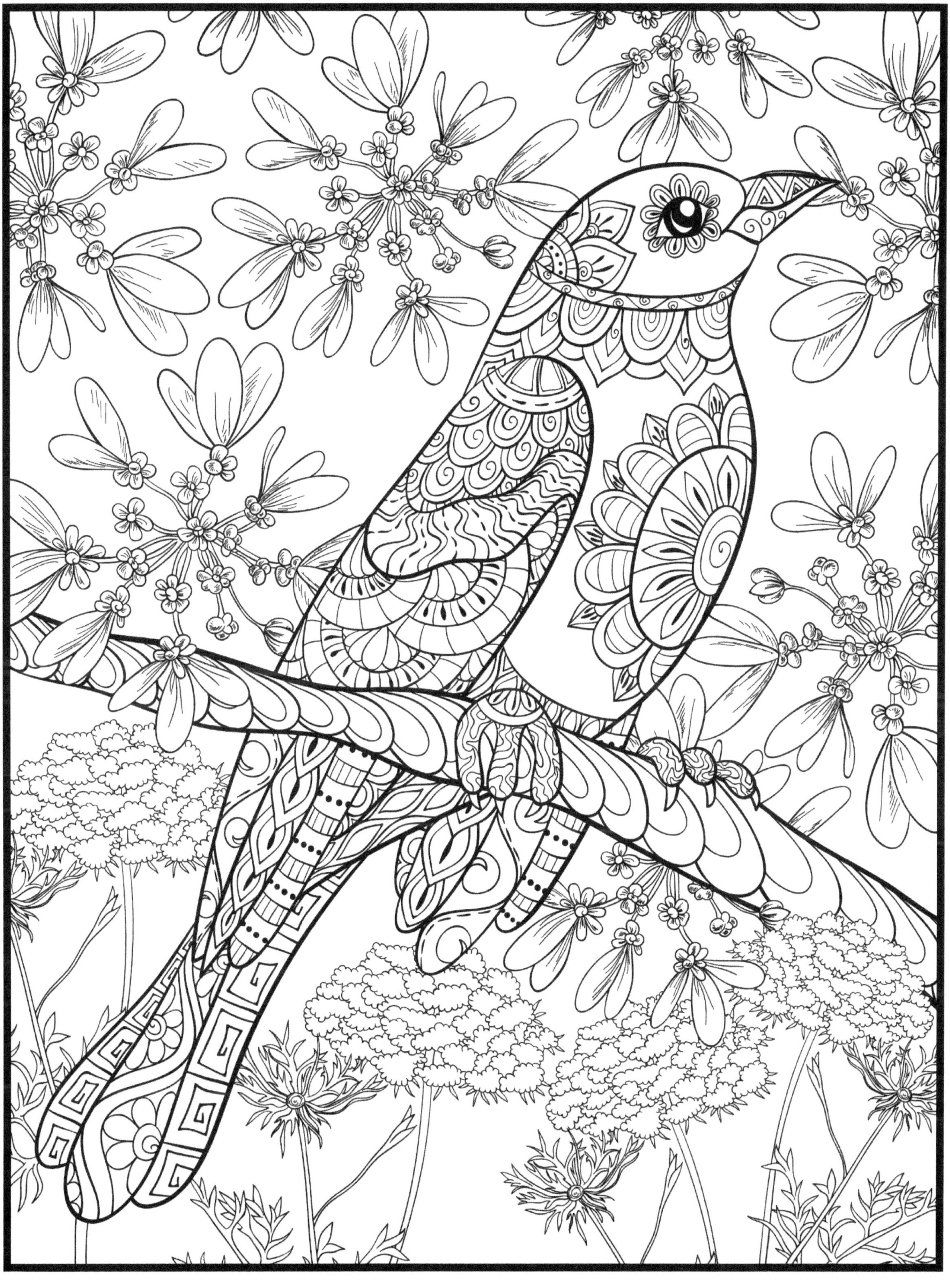

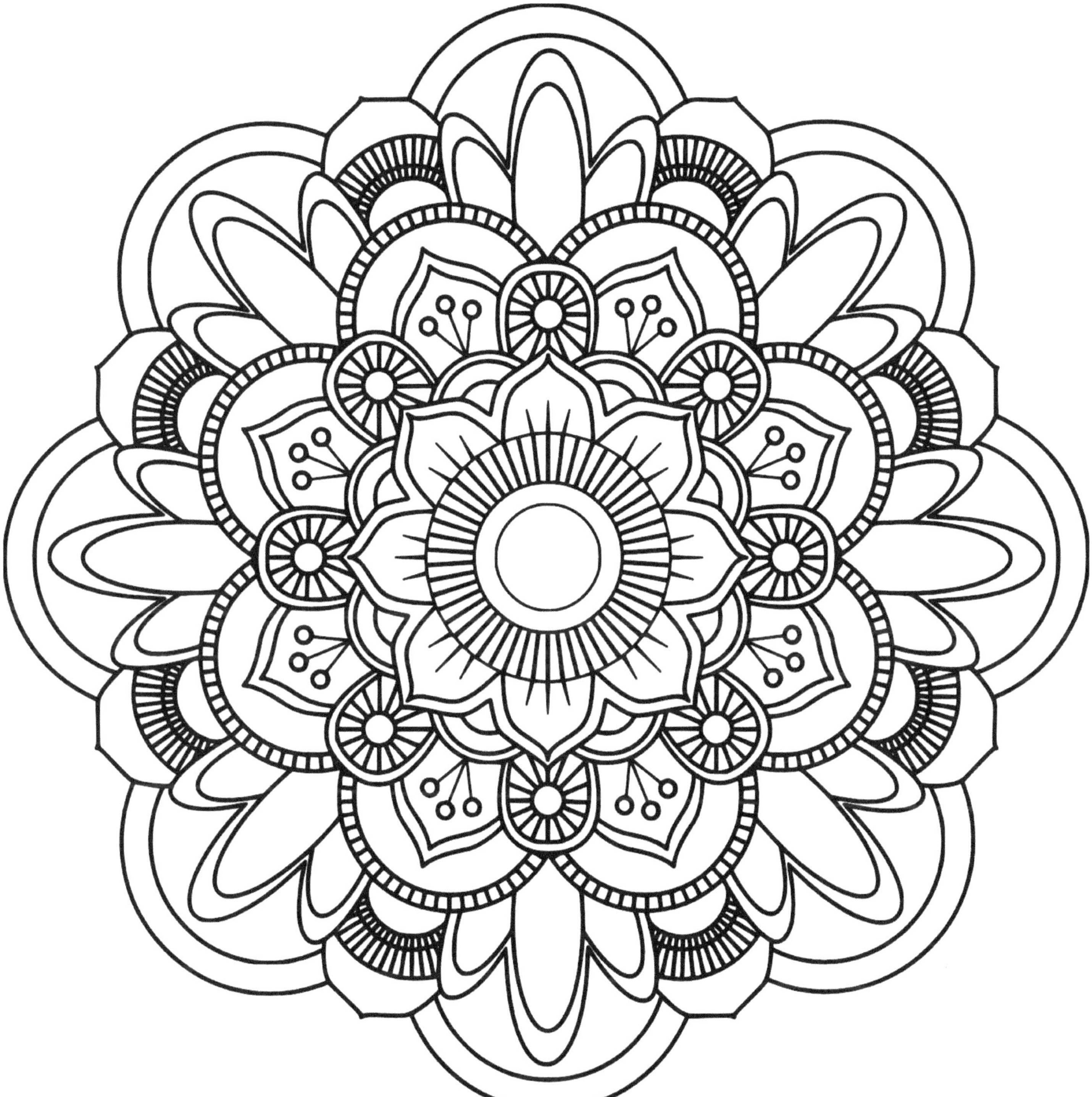

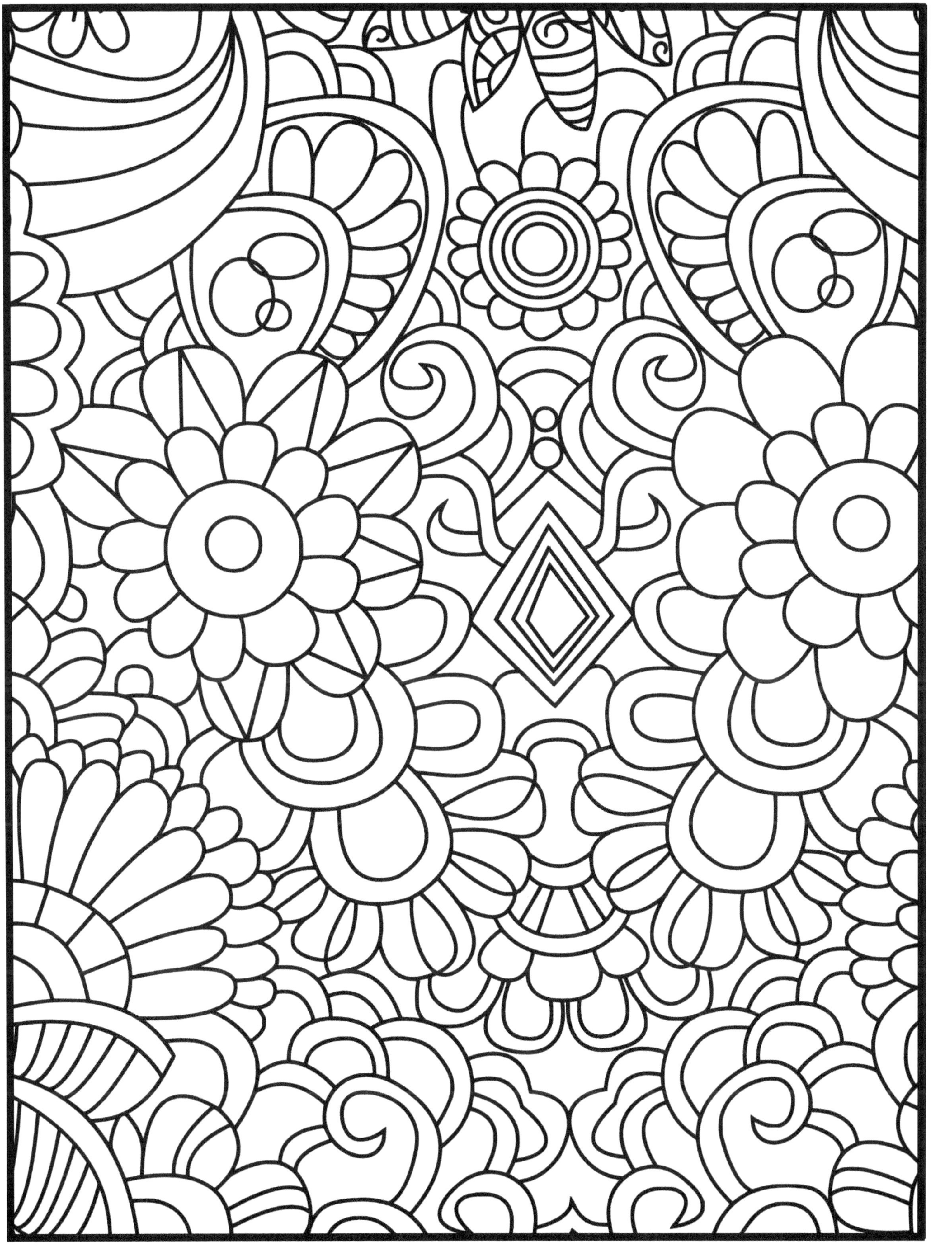

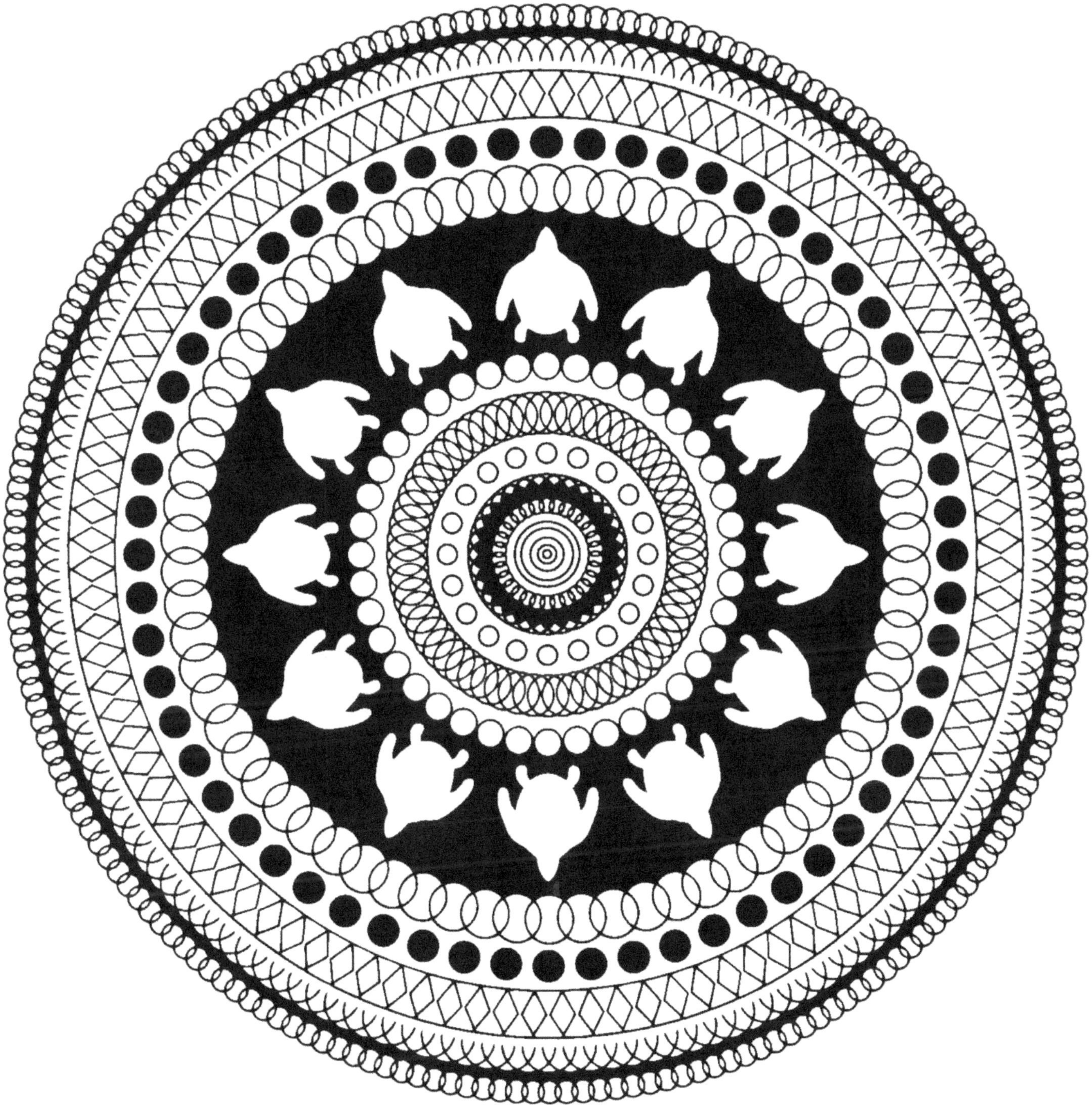

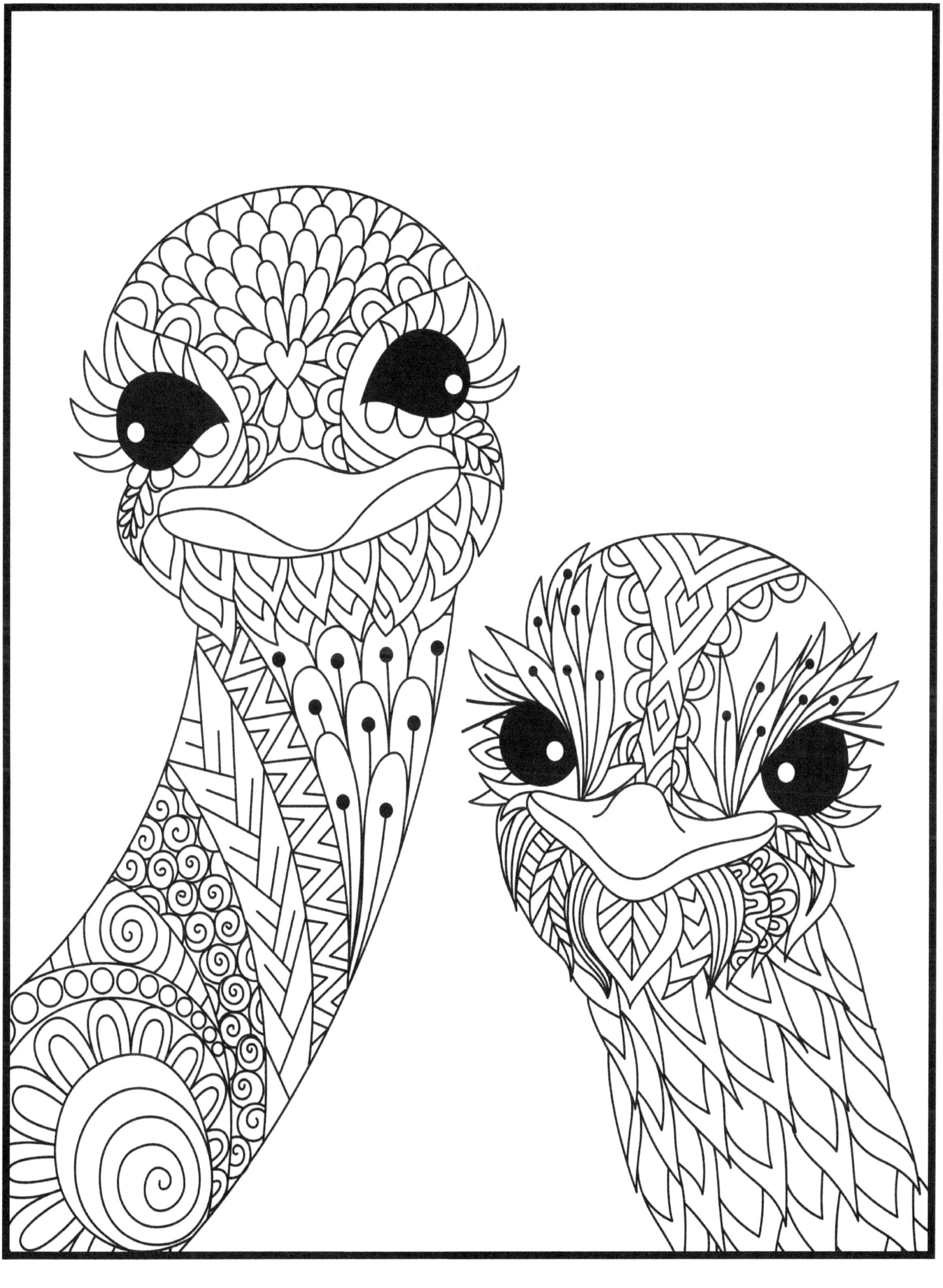

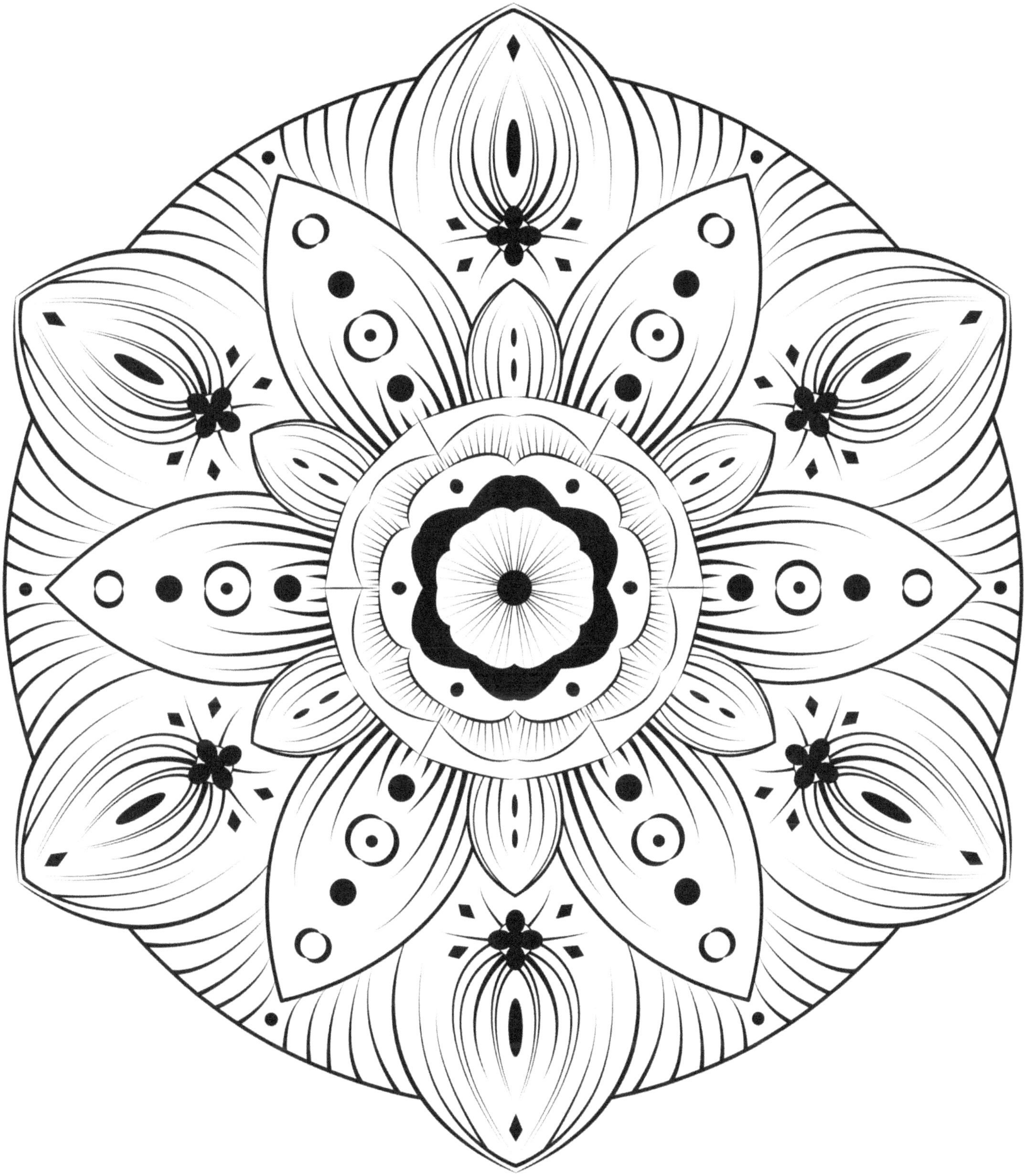

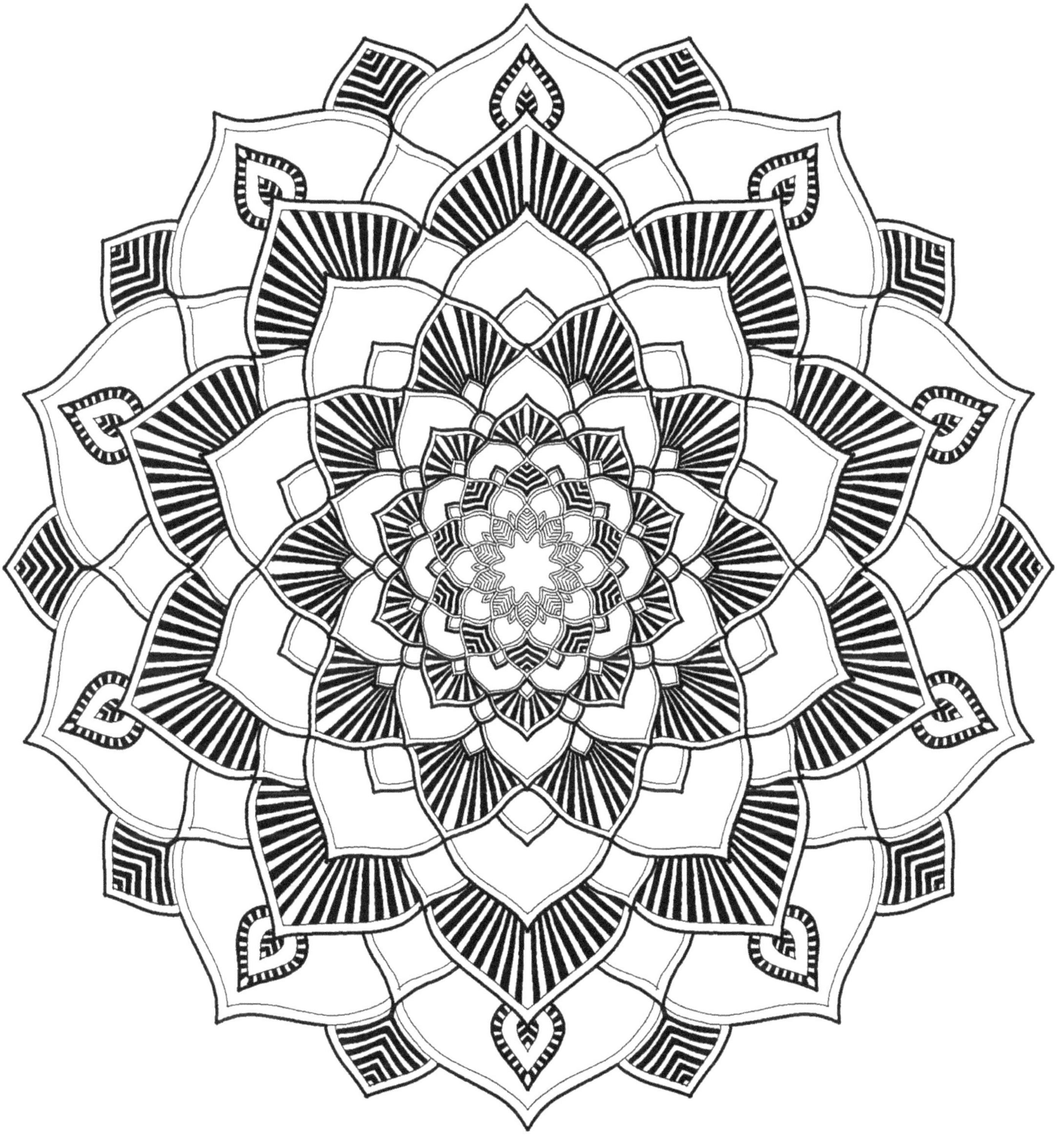

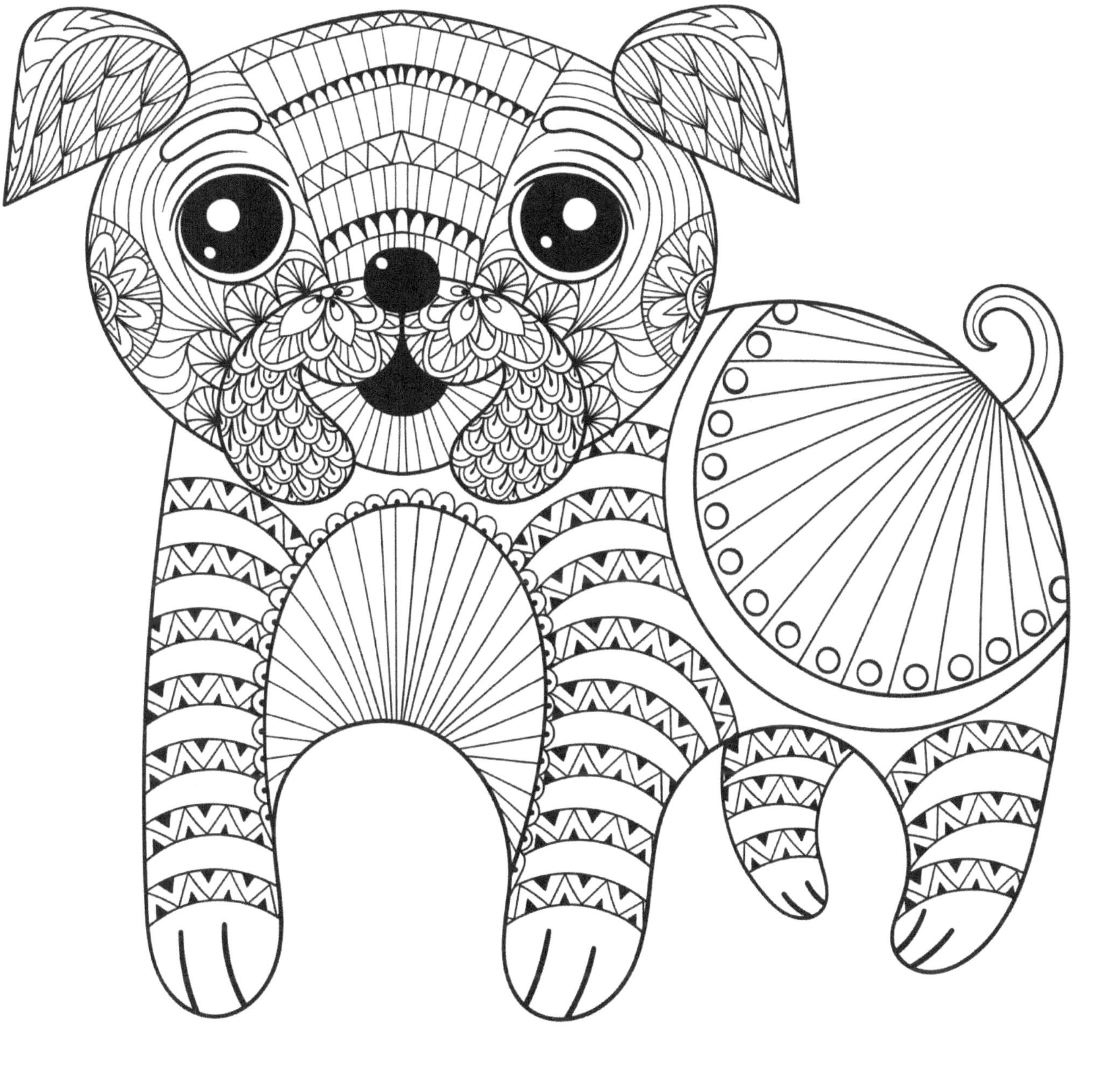

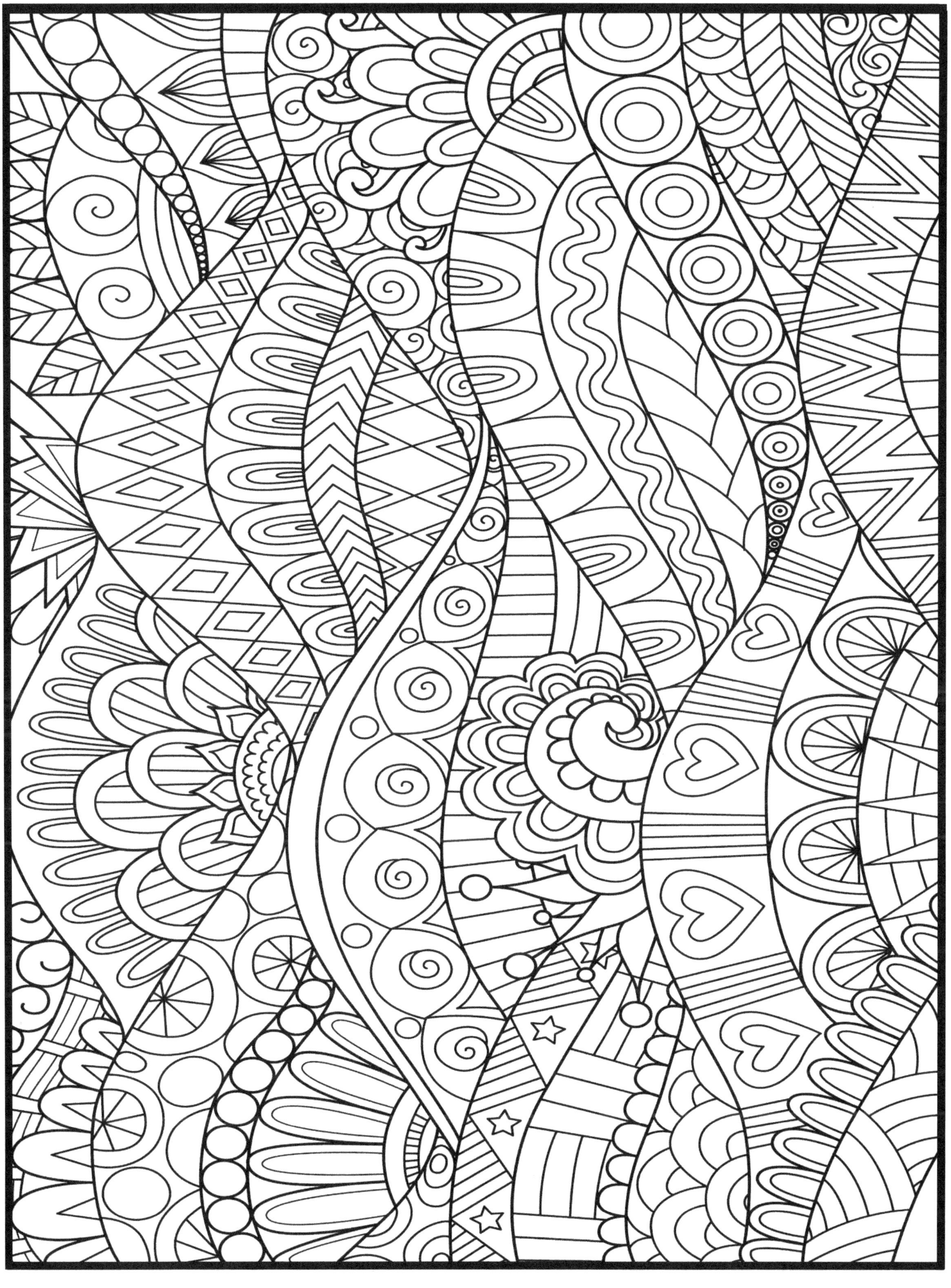

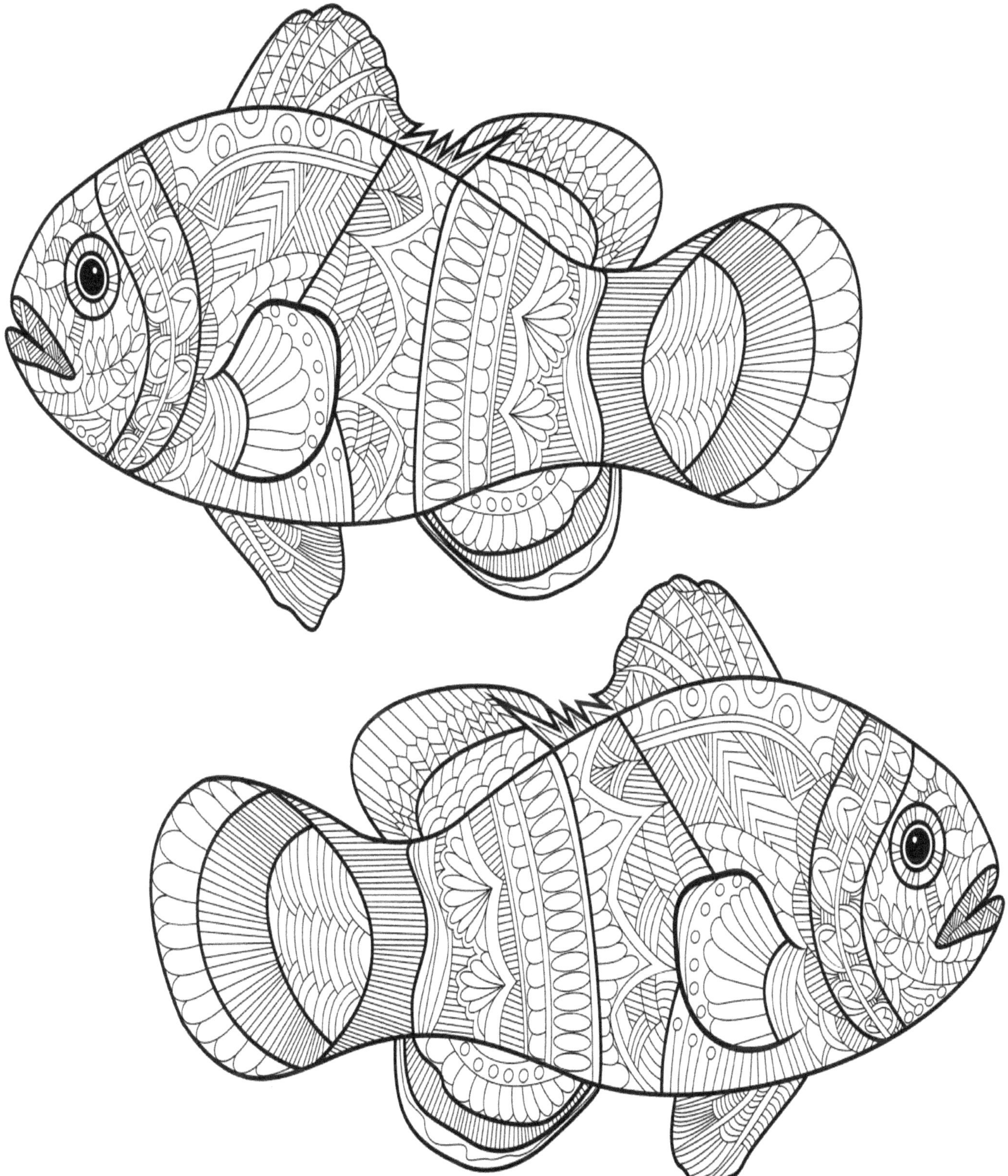

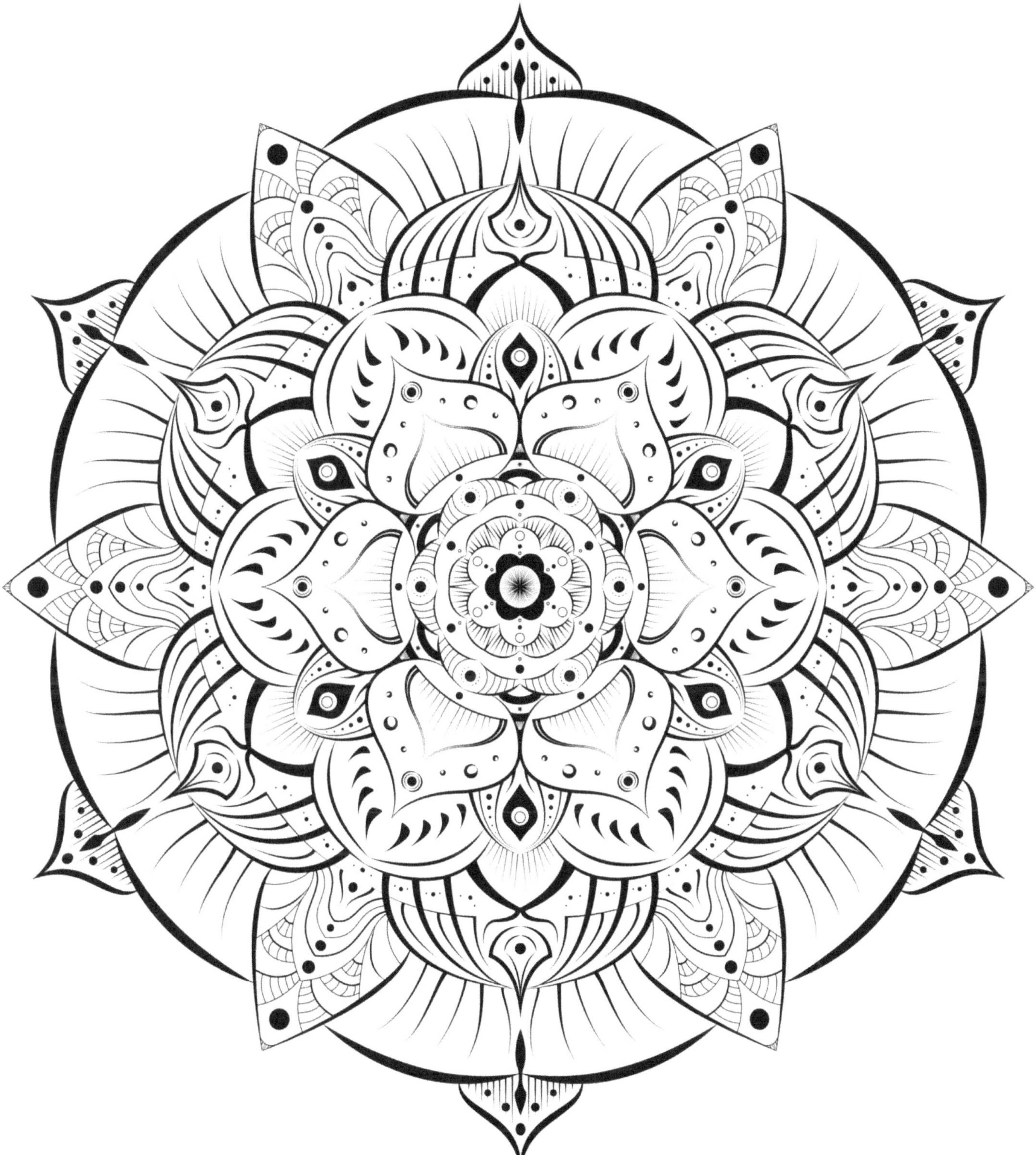

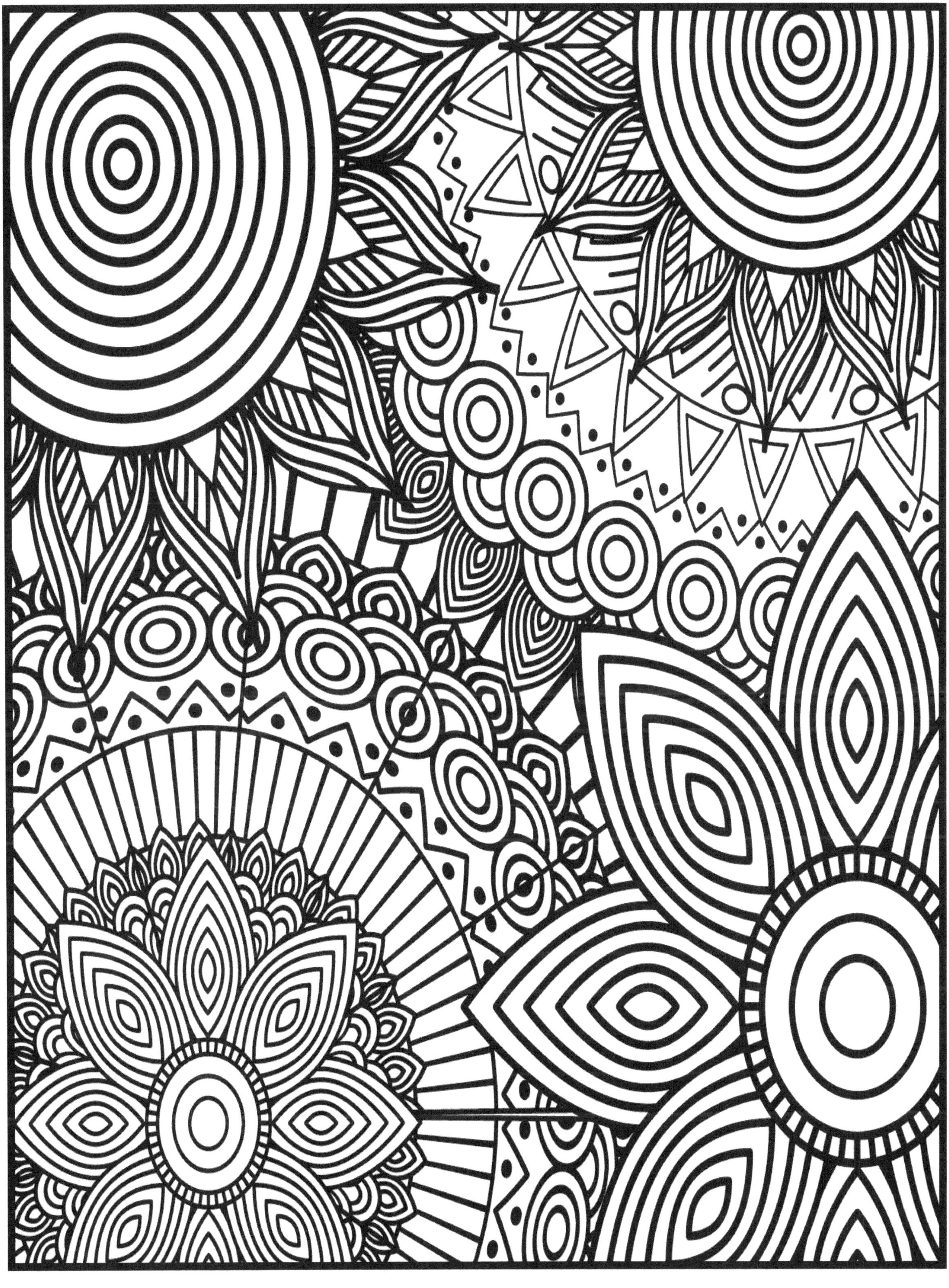

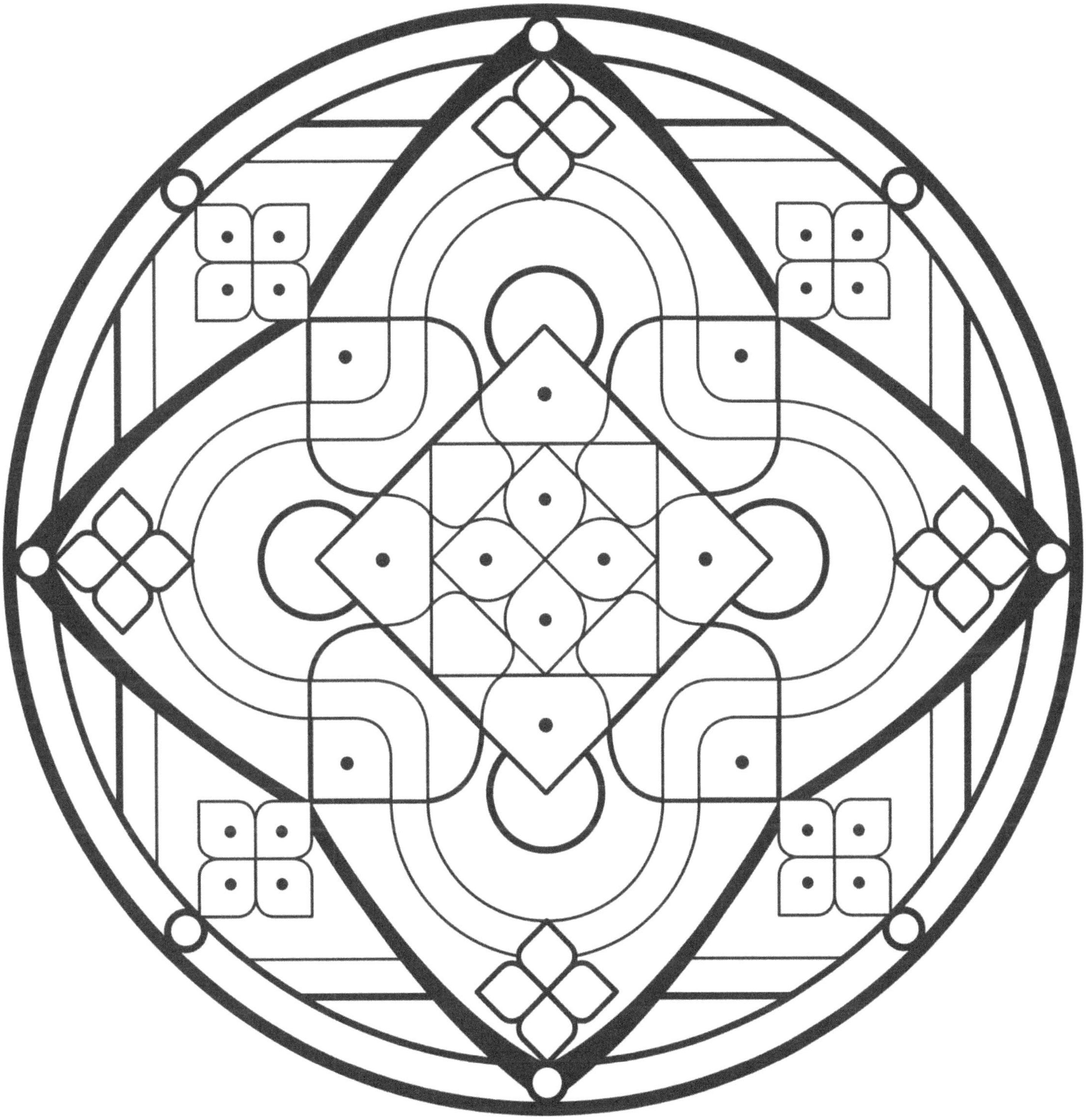

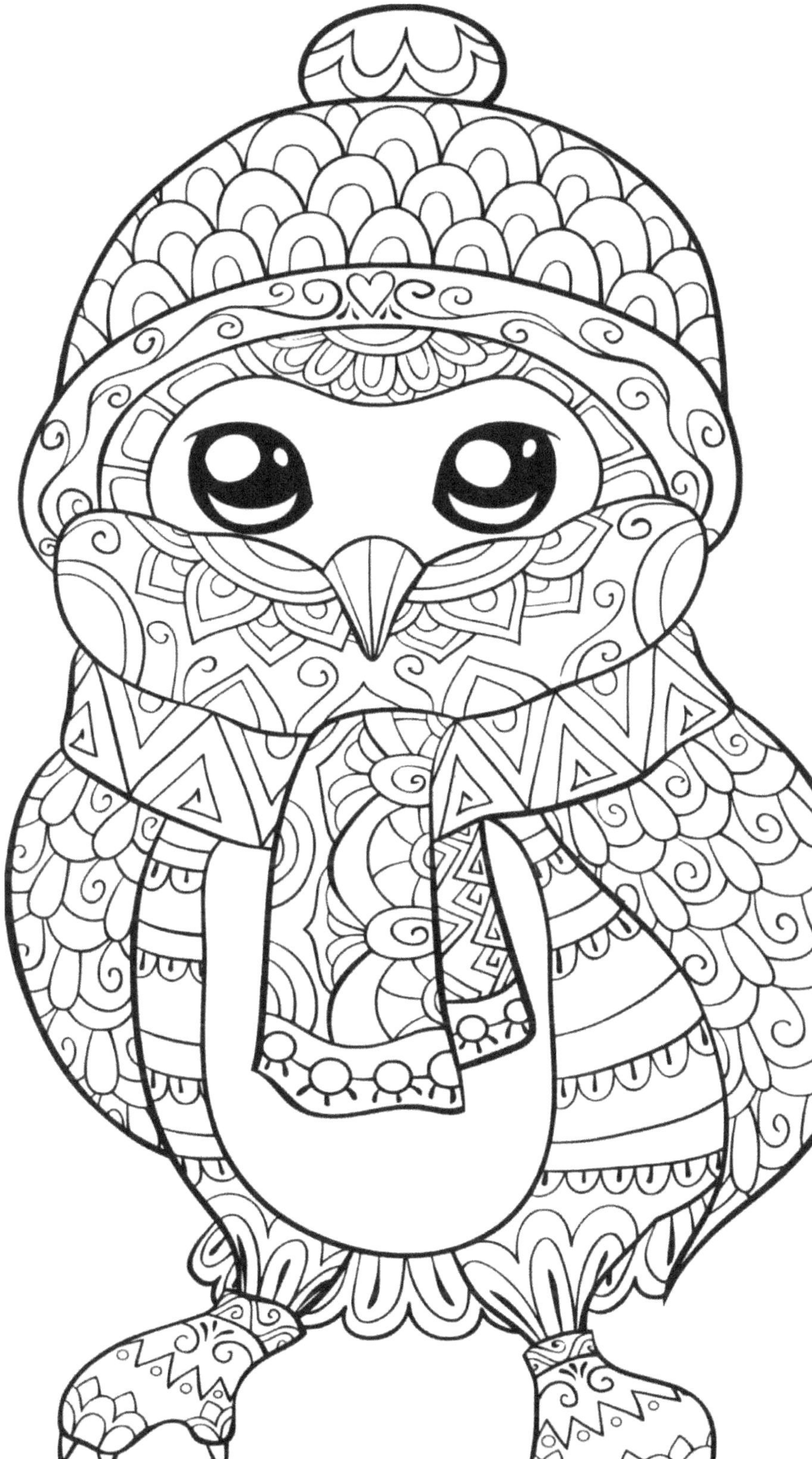

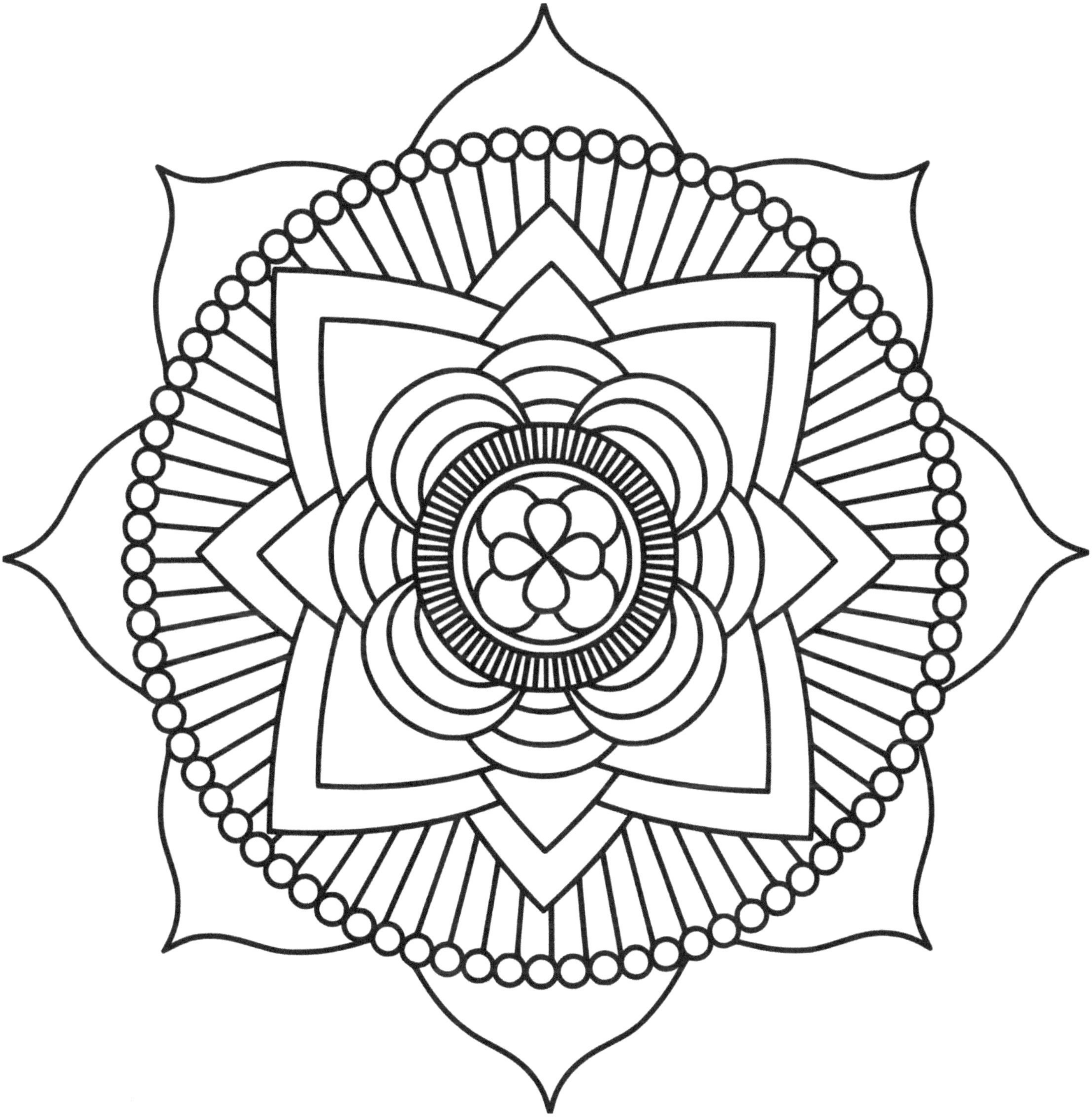

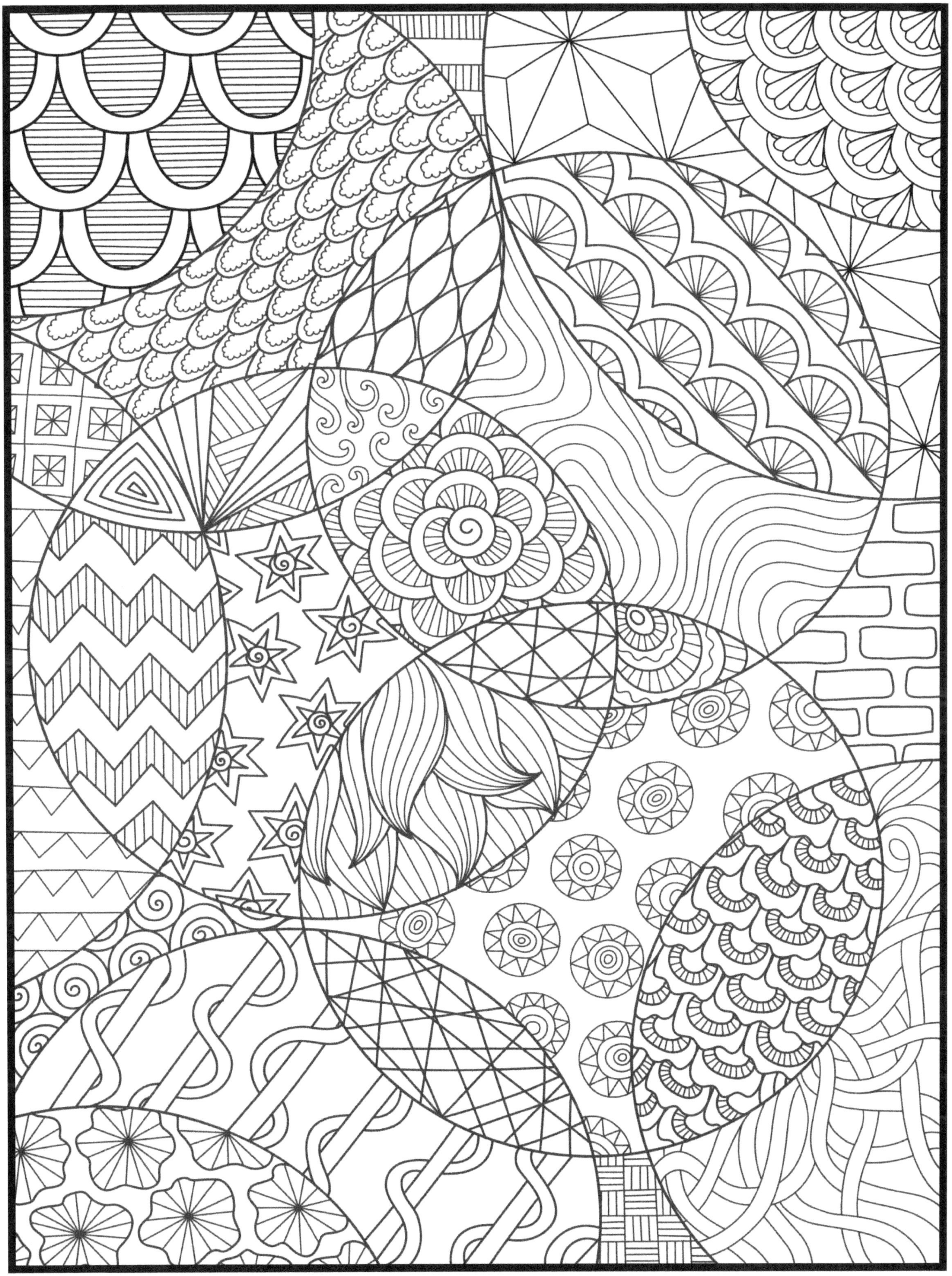

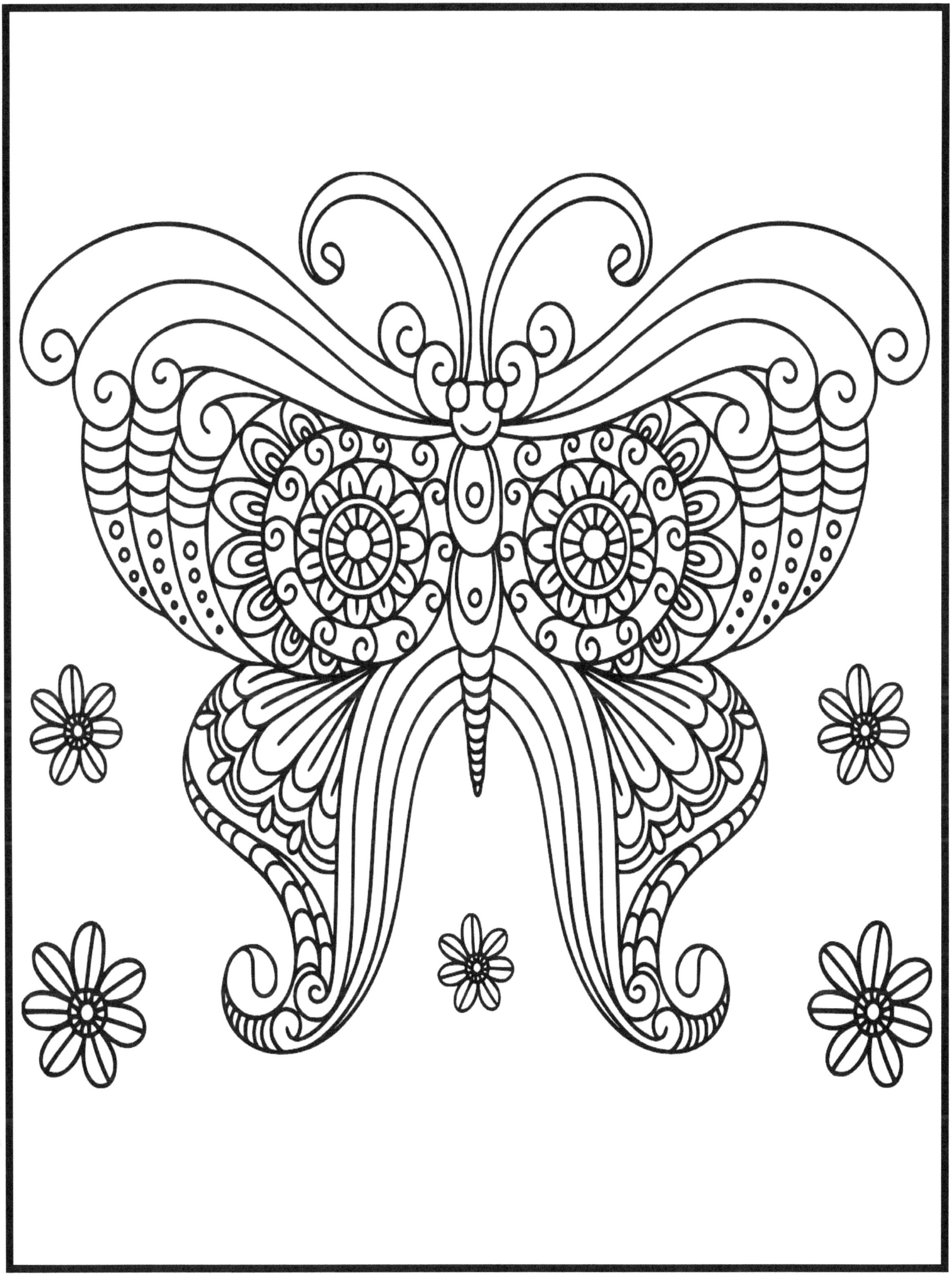

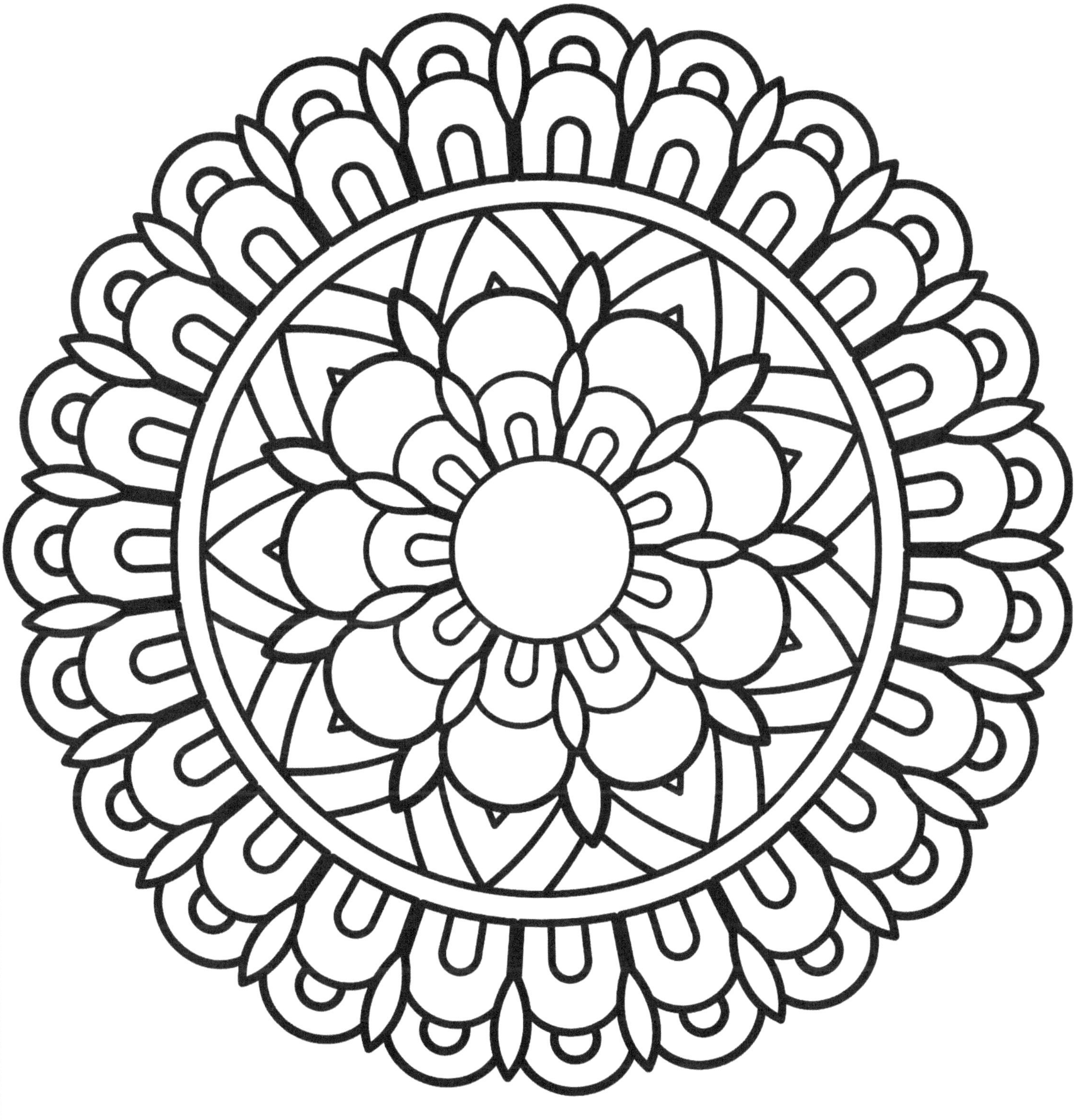

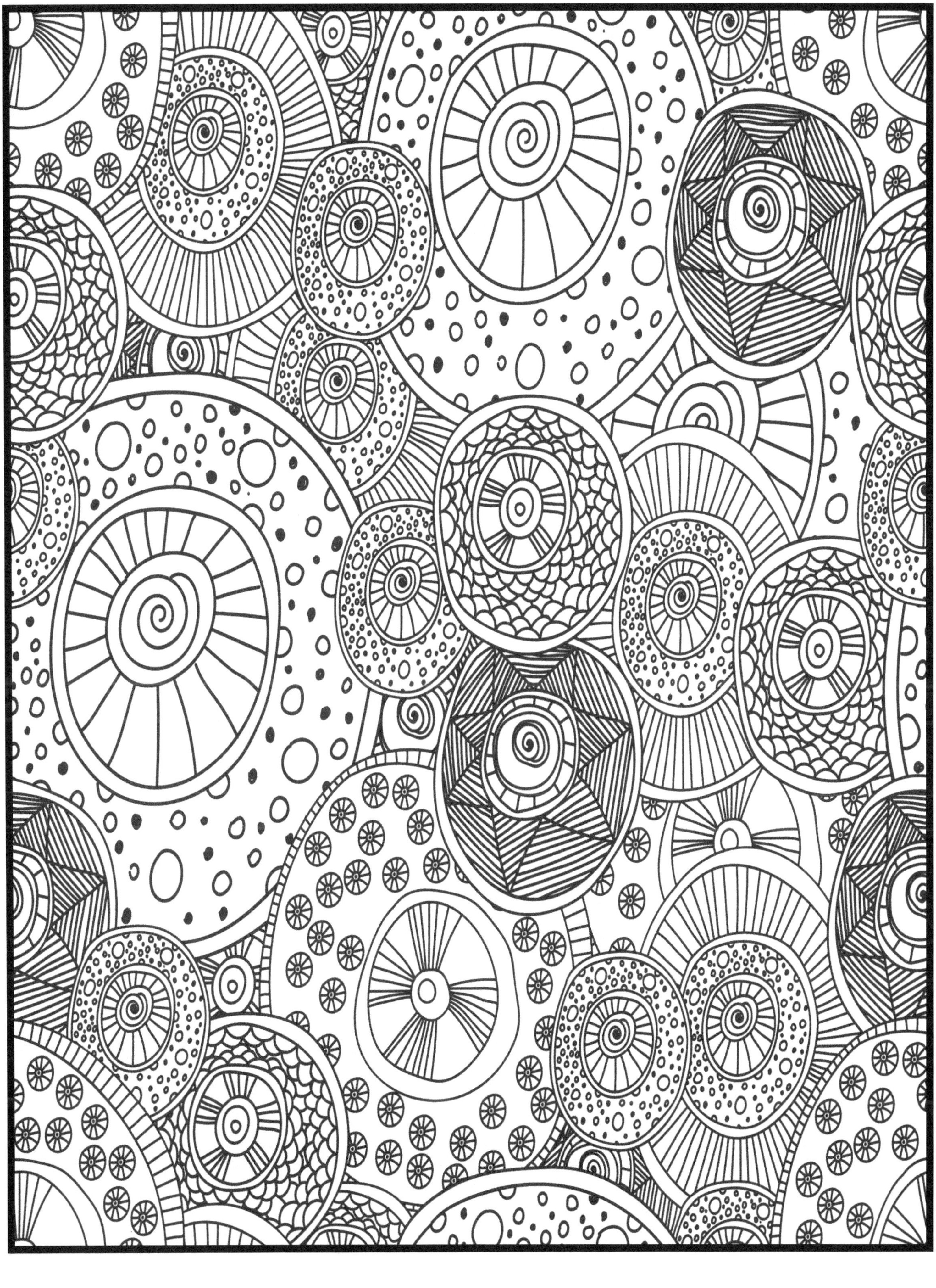

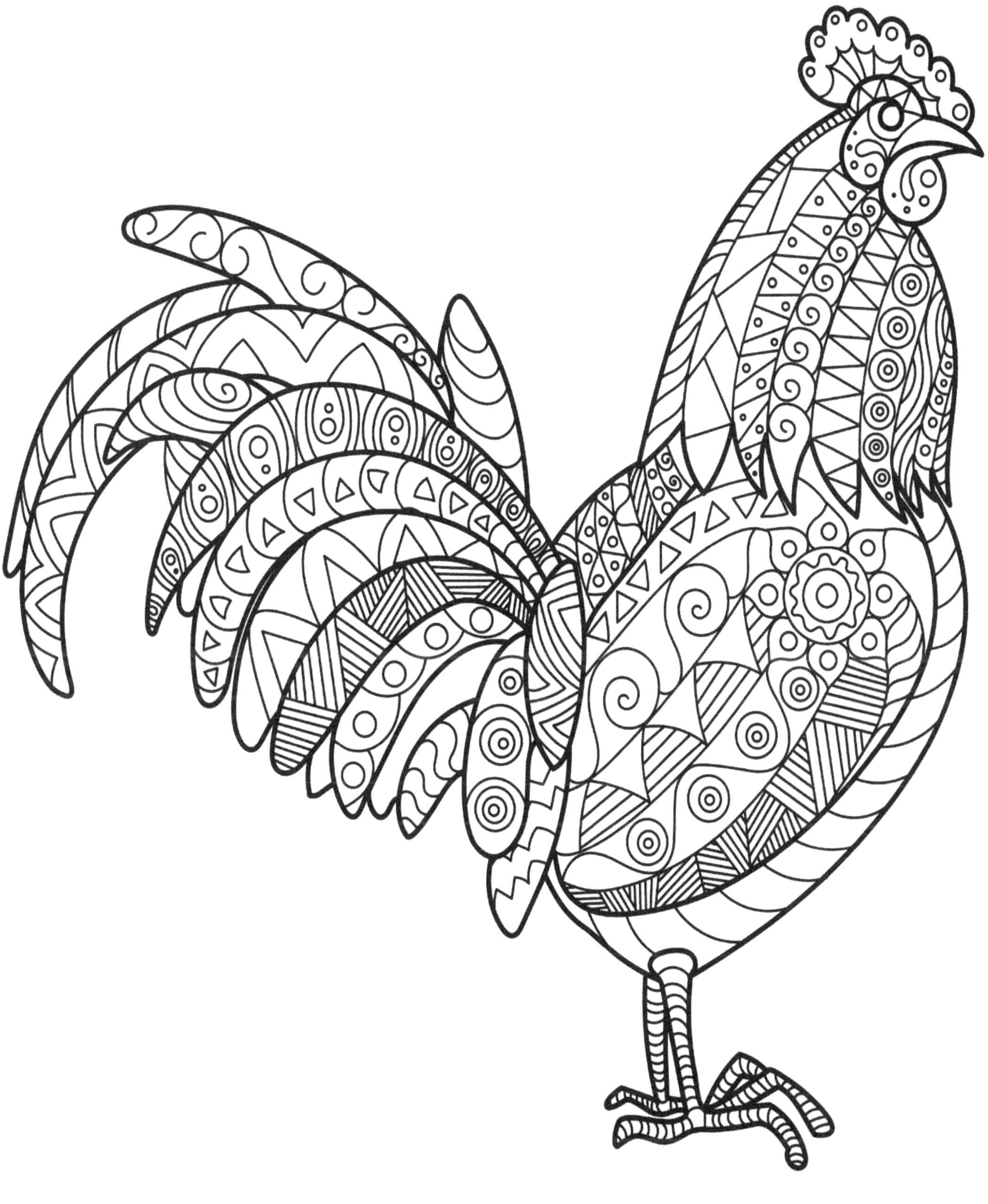

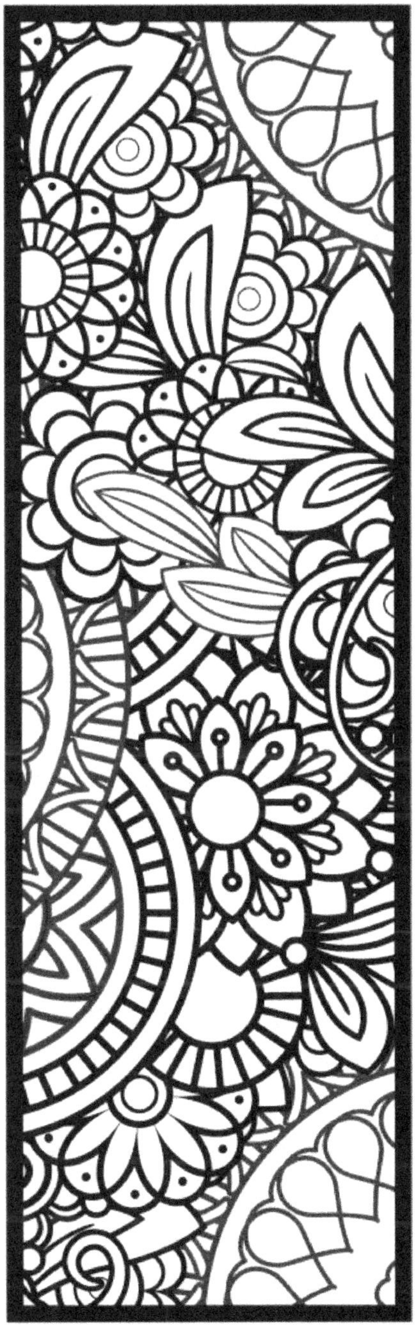
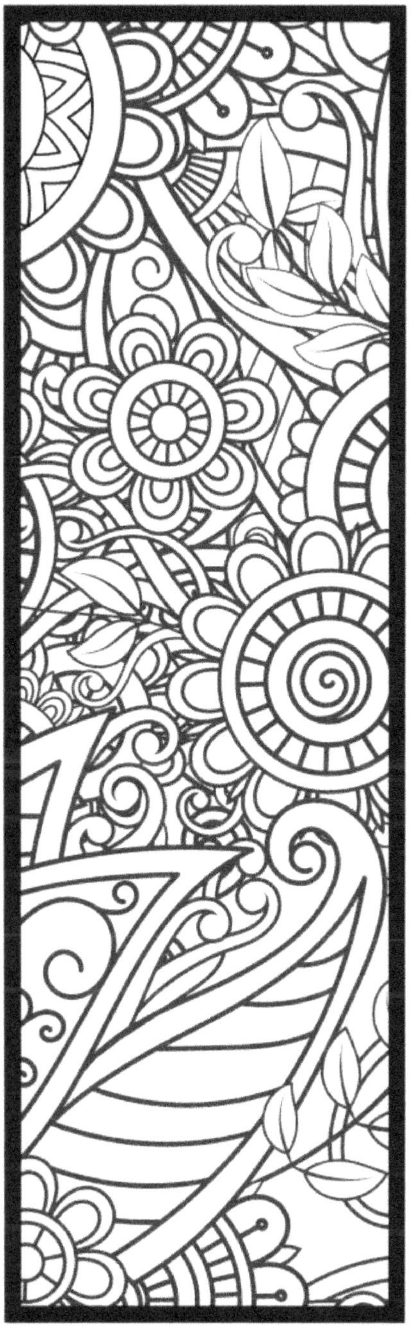

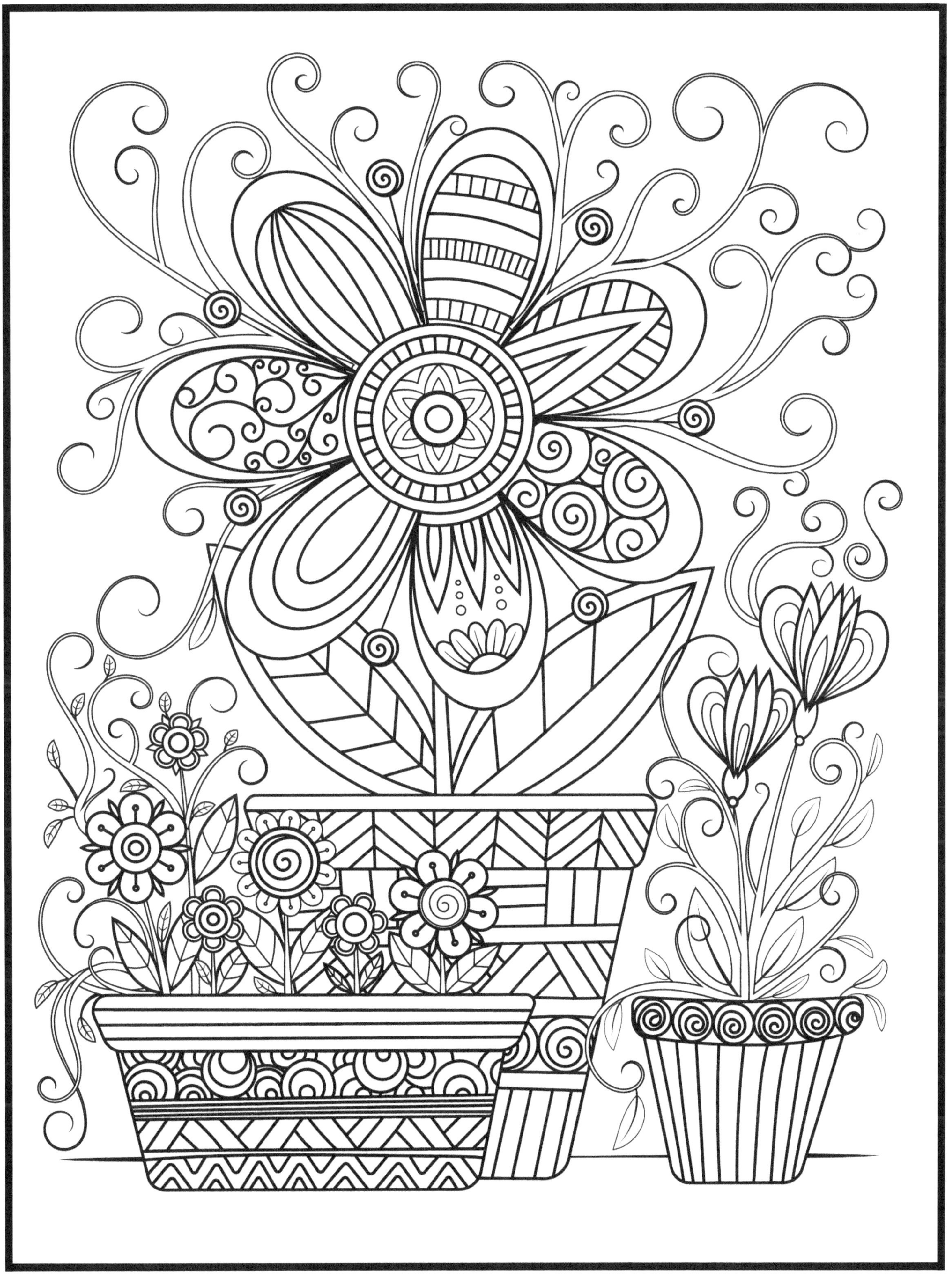

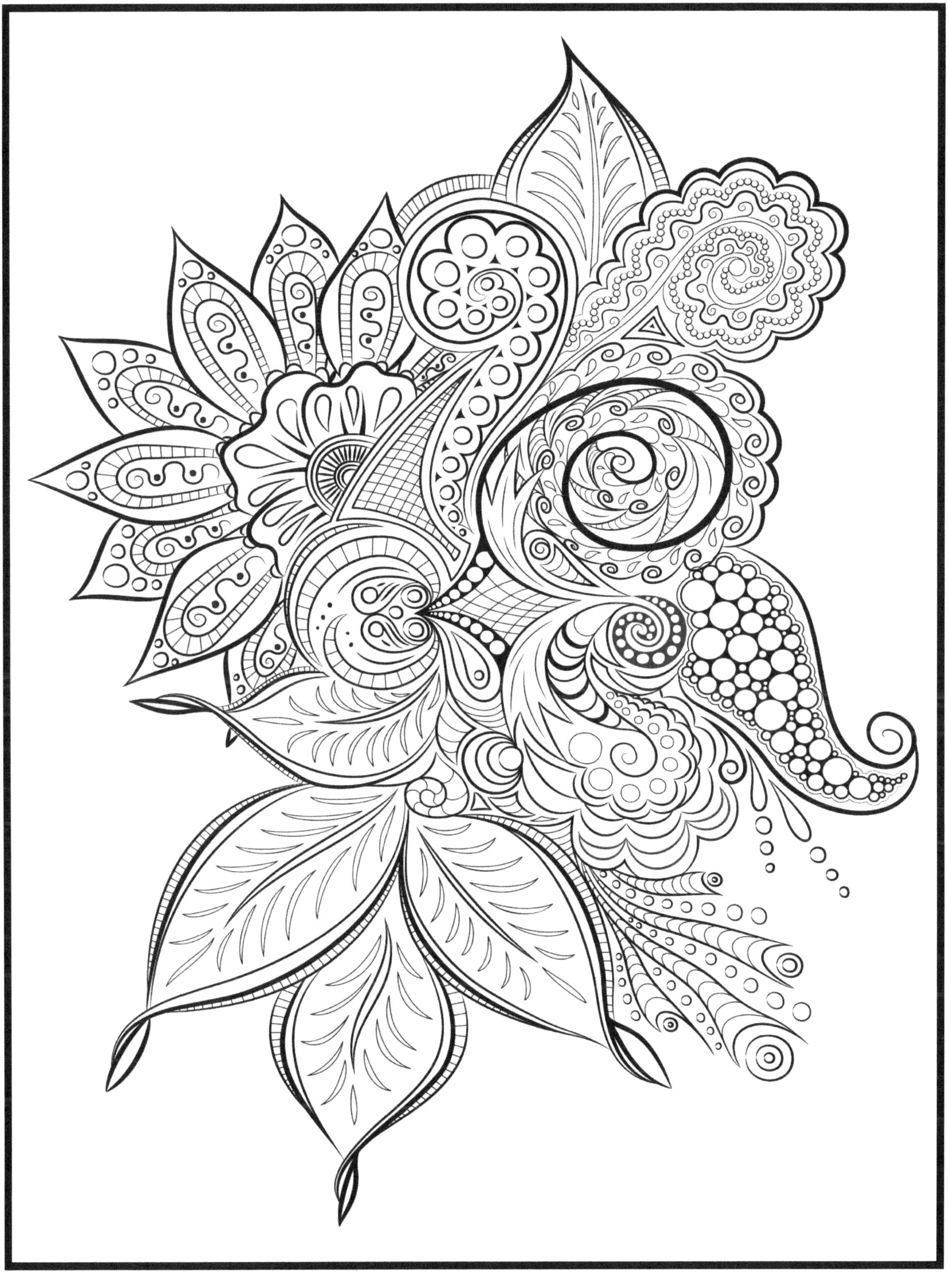

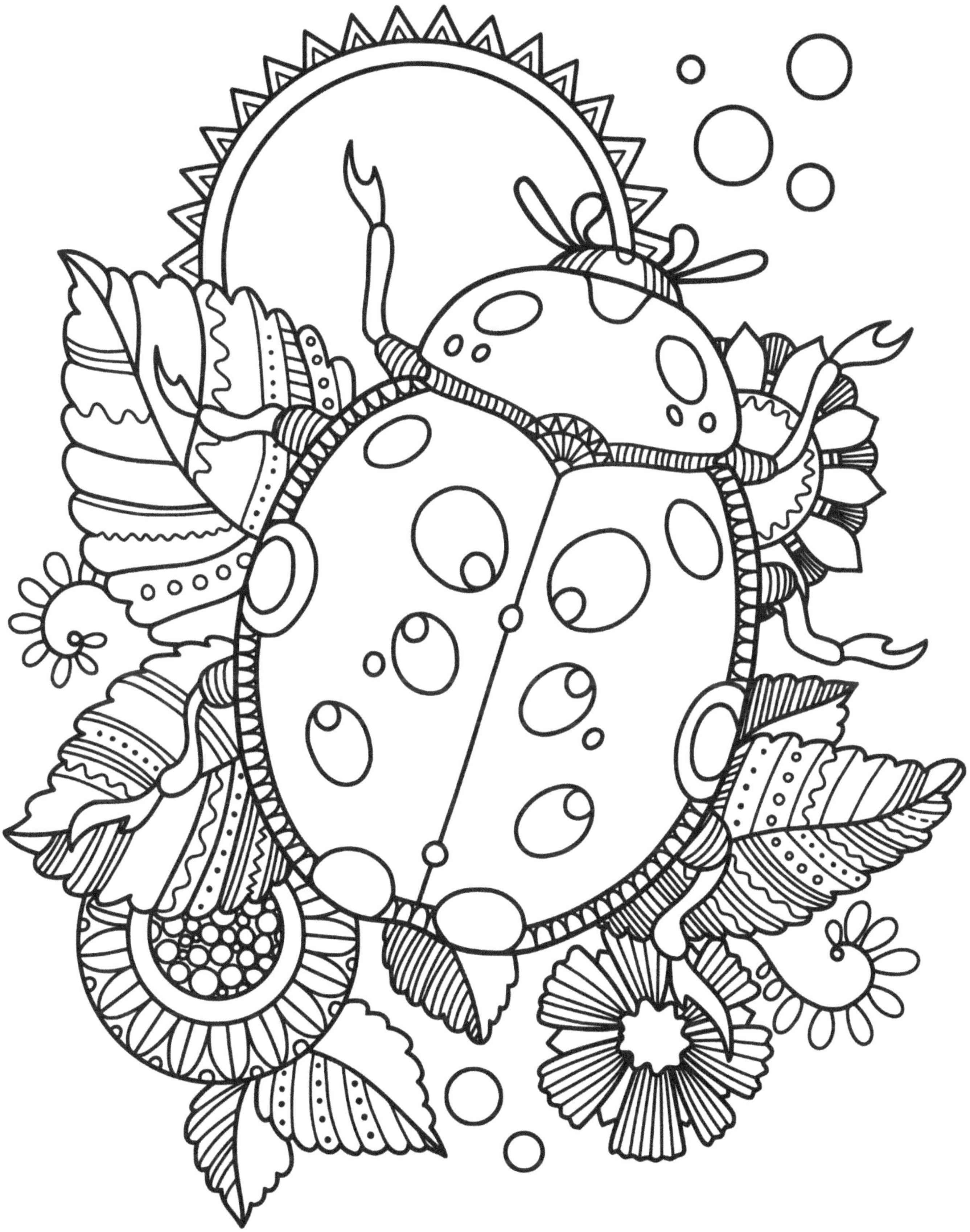

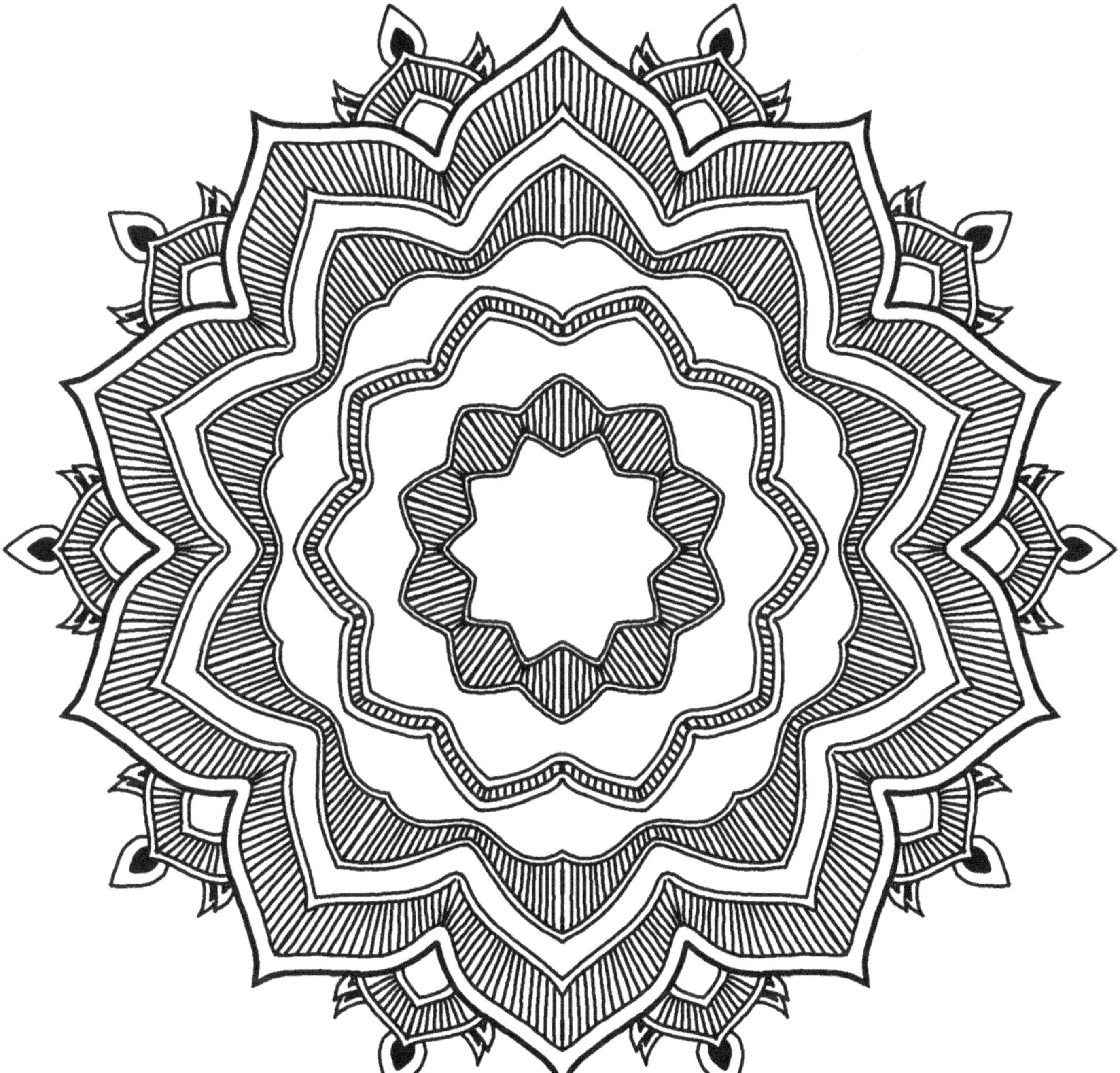

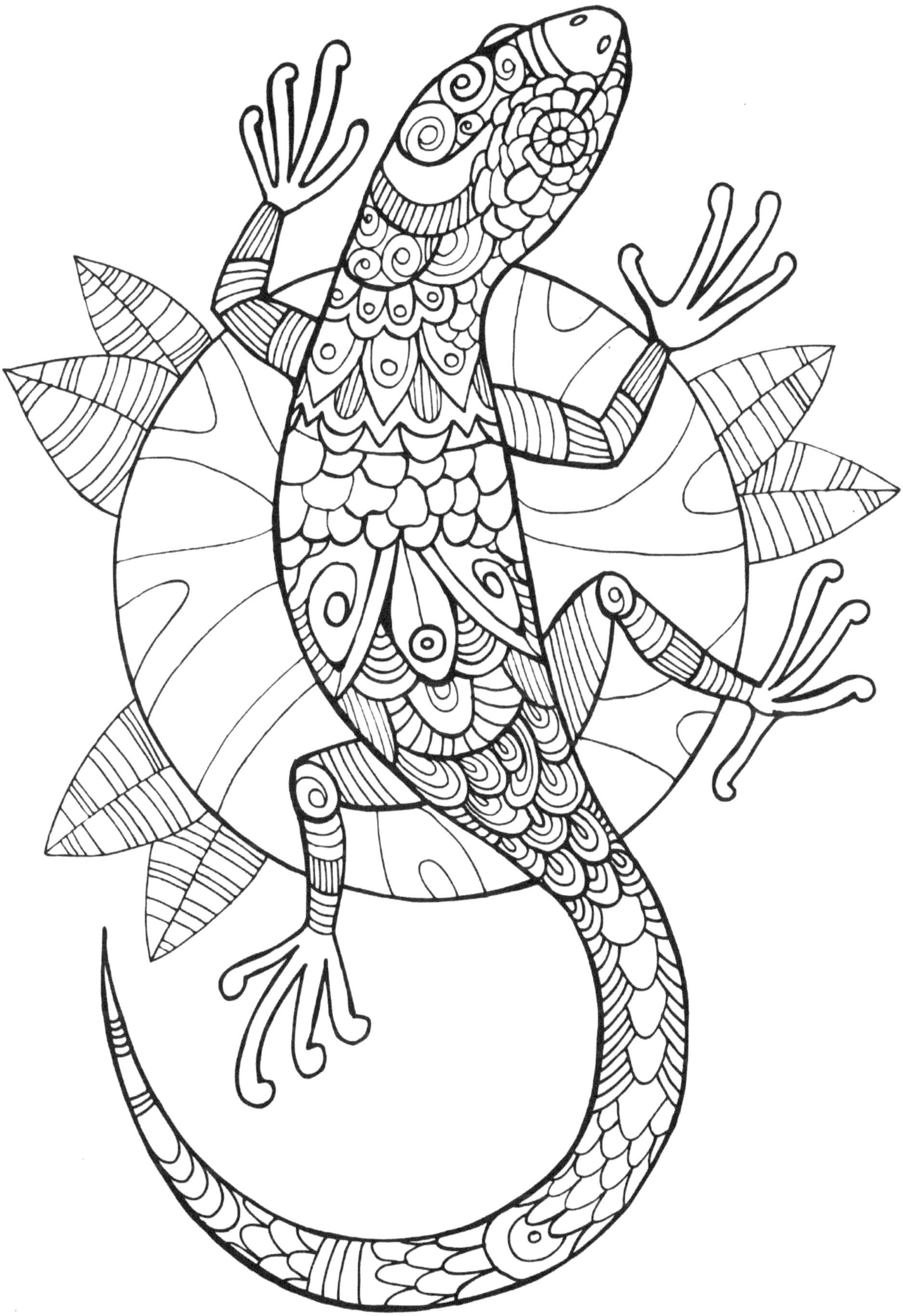

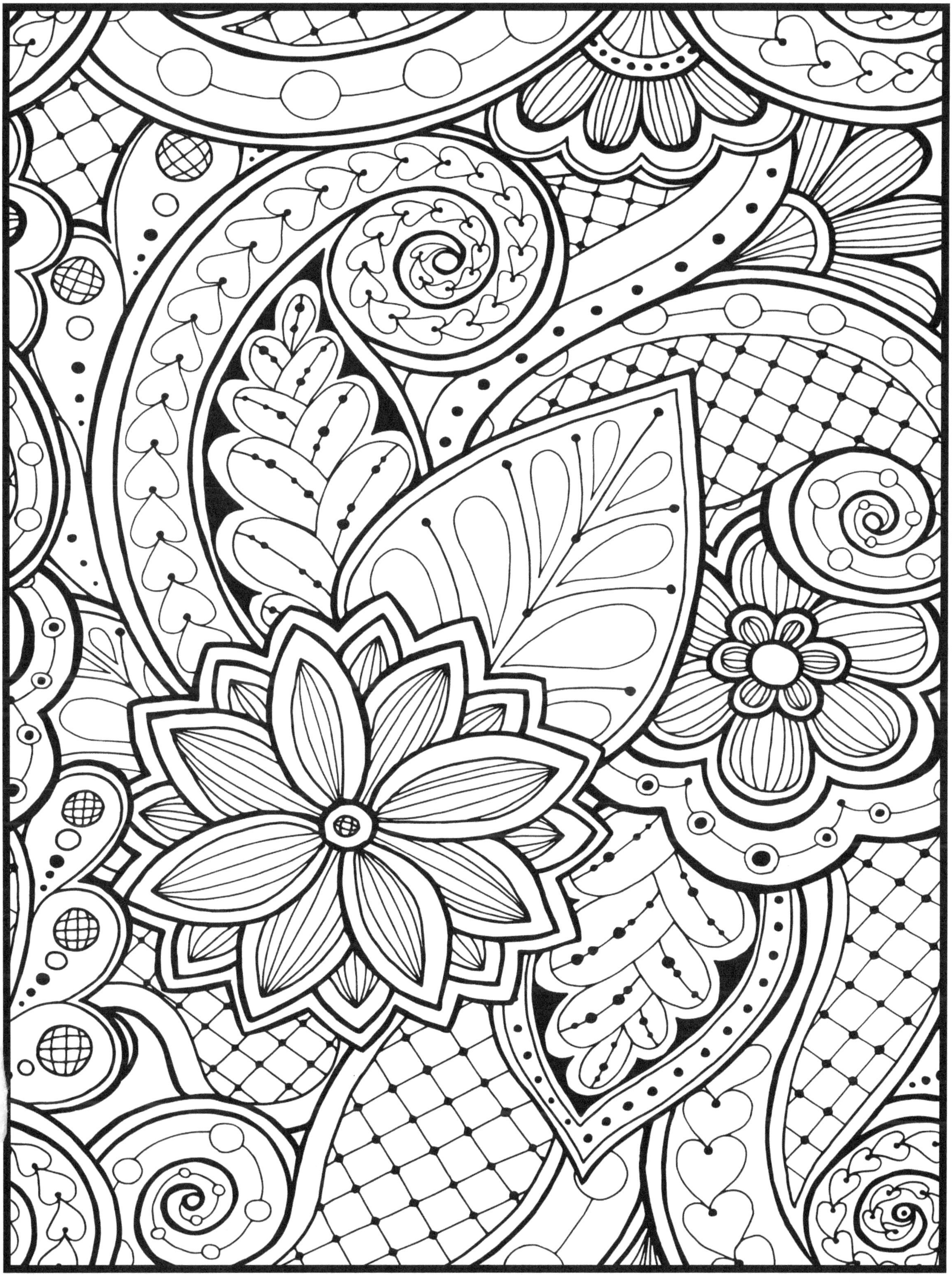